150

MASTER STROKES

MASTER STROKES

SPIRITUAL GROWTH THROUGH
THE GAME OF GOLF

GARY D. YORK & KEN OSNESS

TYNDALE HOUSE PUBLISHERS, INC. • WHEATON, ILLINOIS

Library of Congress Cataloging-in-Publication Data

York, Gary, date
  Master strokes / Gary York and Ken Osness.
    p. cm.
  Includes bibliographical references.
  ISBN 0-8423-3592-7
  1. Golfers—Religious life. 2. Golf—Religious aspects—Christianity. 3. Christian life. I. Osness, Ken, date II. Title.

BV4596.G64 Y67 2000
248.8'8—dc21   99-086450

Printed in the United States of America.

06 05 04 03 02 01 00
7   6   5   4   3   2   1

CONTENTS

Introduction

Like millions of other people in America, we are avid golfers. But while we love the game, we are far from good—the Holy Land is the only "tour" we will be seeing anytime soon. As the old saying goes, "We shoot in the 70s, but if it gets much colder than that, we don't play." The truth is that on the rare occasions when our scores do slip into the 70s, we feel as if we're getting a foretaste of heaven. Excitement reigns at this apparent confirmation that we're improving.

Golf is a great passion in both of our lives. But we've found that enhancing our play is a slow, difficult, and deliberate process—very similar to the process involved in another great passion of our lives: becoming more like Jesus. In fact, the discovery that these two great passions are so similar is what inspired us to write this book.

Like our Christian faith, golf is a big part of what we are. I (Gary) started playing the game as a young boy shortly after I became a Christian. The municipal golf course in my hometown of Beloit, Wisconsin, was adjacent to the swimming pool. Between golf and swimming, I could fill my whole day. In the mornings, I'd pay twenty-five cents to play nine holes of golf, using my dad's clubs, wooden shafts and all. After a short walk home and a brief lunch of macaroni and cheese, I could return and spend my afternoon at the pool for a dime. My golf game has been growing alongside my Christian life ever since those idyllic summer days.

I (Ken) didn't start playing golf until much later in life. Gary and I had been working together on the ministry staff at Eastview Christian Church in Bloomington, Illinois, for six years when Gary planned a staff retreat that included golf as a team-building activity. One of two staff members who didn't know how to golf, I borrowed clubs from a friend and let the rest of the staff know that I expected to have great fun learning the game. For my first experience, they took me out for thirty-six holes in hundred-degree heat. It was a baptism by fire, as they say. I was exhausted when I was done, but I finished!

Both of us are hooked on golf. We have become intense students of the game—including its history. We've learned, for example, that one of the first historical references to golf was during the reign of King James II of Scotland in 1457. Apparently, the game had become so popular that the king was afraid it was putting the country at risk in its ongoing war with England. It was interfering with his soldiers' archery practice, so he persuaded the Scottish parliament to ban the game. Golf was played early in the history of America; the first country clubs in the

U.S., the South Carolina Club and the Savannah Club, were opened in the late 1700s. It has become so popular in this country that in 1996, 442 new golf courses opened in the U.S.

We not only love to play golf and research its history, we love to ponder the many parallels between the game and life, and in particular, the spiritual life. As you'll learn in this book, living a life that is pleasing to God is a lot like playing golf: We have to handle ups and downs, recover from our mistakes, stay away from hazards, deal with our handicaps, overcome bad habits, develop positive attitudes, and build lasting relationships. Fortunately, in real life, we can claim God as our playing partner, instructor, encourager, rehabilitator, and role model.

Your tee time awaits you in chapter one. Keep the ball in play and your life in Christ.

Gary York and Ken Osness

xi

I don't have a handicap—I'm all handicap.
Lyndon Johnson

CHAPTER

Knowing Your Handicap:
RECOGNIZING YOUR LIMITATIONS

> *I was given the gift of a handicap to
> keep me in constant touch with my lim-
> itations. . . . At first I didn't think of it
> as a gift and begged God to remove it.
> [But God said] . . . 'My strength comes
> into its own in your weakness.'*
> 2 CORINTHIANS 12:7–9
> (*The Message*)

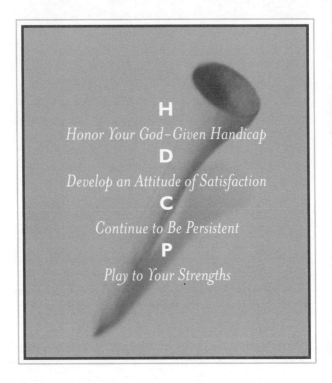

H
Honor Your God-Given Handicap

D
Develop an Attitude of Satisfaction

C
Continue to Be Persistent

P
Play to Your Strengths

ave you ever heard the term "to lionize"? It means to elevate someone to a level of great importance. If you "lionize" someone, you recognize him or her as being almost bigger than life. In 1996 a twenty-year-old stepped from golf's amateur ranks to join the PGA Tour. Though barely more than a teenager, he seemed bigger than life. After winning his third consecutive United States amateur title and finishing his sophomore year at Stanford University, he decided to turn pro.

When Nike signed him to a $40 million endorsement deal, he was labeled the next superstar before ever teeing up as a pro. In his first eight tournaments he carded two victories and three top-five finishes, banked $855,000 in earnings, and earned a player's exemption for 1997. No one has captured the center stage of golf like this since a young Jack Nicklaus took the sport by storm in the early 1960s. Considered by many to be the greatest golfer ever, Nicklaus is in a class by himself. Before he began to play the Senior PGA Tour, where he has gained ten victories, he won seventy-three tournaments, including eighteen majors. Six of those victories won him green jackets at the Masters. That's more than any other player. Time will tell us if his stunning records will be eclipsed by the mastery of Tiger Woods.

3

George Peper, editor of *Golf Magazine,* once wrote that while the media has lionized Tiger Woods, his stellar performance has "Tigerized" most other golfers. In other words, Tiger's skill and performance on the golf course make the rest of us look like hockey players. At age three, while most of us were breaking into Mom's cookie jar, Tiger was breaking fifty on nine holes at his hometown golf course.

Many of us look at Tiger Woods and describe his golf game as flawless. We see a man with no handicap and no limitations. But if you were to ask him, he could describe them with technical precision and clarity. While we can't see them, he can. He knows his handicap, recognizes his limitations—and flourishes within them.

What's your handicap—in golf and in life? We all have at least one thing that we would describe as a limitation to doing well. But a handicap doesn't have to be viewed as something negative. As a matter of fact, it can be a very positive thing in golf. When each player's score is adjusted according to his handicap—the average number of strokes that player shoots over par—a novice can play with an expert without feeling intimidated. If we took into account our handicaps, the two of us could play with Tiger Woods or Jack Nicklaus and be competitive! In any case, we can enjoy the game so much more by recognizing our limitations and playing within them. Acknowledging a handicap lowers expectations, lessens stress, and increases the fun.

While we don't know our official handicaps on the golf course, we pretty much know what our limitations are. As a result, we don't expect to shoot par on every hole. We know that we will have some good shots and some bad shots, usually more bad than good. We will have some good holes and some bad holes, often more bad than good. Neither of us throws clubs, curses at the ball, has headaches, or wonders why we keep playing the game. We want to improve, and we have moments of disappointment, but we rarely get stressed over it. Former president Gerald Ford had a good perspective on this issue, saying, "I know I'm getting better at golf because I'm hitting fewer spectators." He wasn't kidding.

Knowing our handicap is valuable in golf, but it is essential in life. No two of us are exactly alike. Our physical, psychological, emotional, and intellectual abilities are different because of the genetic pool from which they were conceived. The speed at which we each process information and adjust to the multi-faceted challenges that come to us, the experiential and attitudinal grids through which all that information passes—and therefore the conclusions we draw from it—are all different. Some of us have tendencies toward sports, some toward art and literature, some toward mathematics and the sciences, and others toward the trades or business and finance. Our environments and experiences growing up bring differing elements into the maturing process, causing us to be callused and shaped in different places and ways. It takes all of us to form a society, and it takes all of us to form and maintain a growing church.

5

God didn't just make us different from each other. He placed limitations on us, enabling us to excel at some things but not everything. Such limitations—our handicaps—increase our value by creating a need for interdependence with others in the church.

There are no insignificant people. When it comes to our value before God, we are all "lionized"—not "Tigerized."

> The human body has many parts, but the
> many parts make up only one body. So it is
> with the body of Christ. In fact, some of the

parts that seem weakest and least important
are really the most necessary. So God has put
the body together in such a way that extra
honor and care are given to those parts that
have less dignity. This makes for harmony
among the members, so that all the members
care of each other equally. (1 Corinthians
12:12, 22, 24-25)

Under his direction, the whole body is
fitted together perfectly, and each part in its
own special way helps the other parts, so that
the whole body is healthy and growing and
full of love. (Ephesians 4:16, TLB)

6

We want to suggest to you that our handicaps—
our limitations—are God designed. We need a wide
variety of people to make life and the church what
God wants them to be. The limitations God has
placed within each of our lives are part of what make
us so valuable. Listen to what the apostle Paul says:

I was given the gift of a handicap to keep me
in constant touch with my limitations. . . . At
first I didn't think of it as a gift, and begged
God to remove it. [But God said to me] . . .
"My strength comes into its own in your
weakness." Once I heard that, I was glad to let
it happen. I quit focusing on the handicap
and began appreciating the gift. It was a case
of Christ's strength moving in on my weakness. Now I take limitations in stride, and

with good cheer, these limitations that cut me
down to size—abuse, accidents, opposition,
bad breaks. I just let Christ take over! And so
the weaker I get, the stronger I become.
(2 Corinthians 12:7-10, *The Message*)

Let's take a look at four suggestions for living with
the God-designed limitations in your life—for
maximizing your H.D.C.P.

Honor Your God-Given Handicap

*Take a good look, friends, at who you were when you got called into
this life. I don't see many of the "brightest and the best" among you,
not many influential, not many from high-society families.*

1 CORINTHIANS 1:26 *(The Message)*

Five PGA tournament winners in 1996 were virtual
"nobodies." They had not won previously on the
tour; their scoring averages put their odds of winning far off the leader board. And yet, the pieces of
their game came together at just the right moment,
enabling them to walk to the winner's circle.

The Masters is golf's most legendary and presti-
gious tournament. All the big and powerful names
in golf capture the limelight as potential winners
each year. But on three occasions the winners have
been virtual rookies, first-time players at the
Augusta National Golf Club—nobodies.

How many times in history has God taken a *nobody* and achieved something monumental with
him?

When God decided to free the children of Israel from bondage in Egypt, he didn't build a secret Israeli guerrilla team to pull a coup and overthrow the government. Instead, he sent a little baby floating down a river in a basket! You may look at that and think, *How stupid. How weak. What kind of plan is that? Why would God do something so strange?* The baby's name was Moses. He grew up to be a guy who thought he couldn't talk well and didn't have the skills to do what God wanted. But God used him to free the Israelites from captivity.

When the children of Israel were being ridiculed and embarrassed by the Philistine army, God sent a small boy with a slingshot to defeat their number one warrior, a nine-foot giant named Goliath. That slingshot-wielding boy was a nobody named David—who later became Israel's greatest king.

When God decided that the children of Israel needed a convincing reminder about being obedient, God chose a young man named Gideon to lead the effort. Gideon thought he had no talent or strength to pull it off, but God selected him anyway. What did he do? No, he didn't put Bibles in all their hotel rooms. After God dismissed more than 22,000 soldiers, Gideon and a small band of 300 warriors made use of the most insignificant implements imaginable—trumpets, clay pots, and torches—to defeat the powerful army of the Midianites.

What we see as insignificant, unusable, even worthless, God sees as powerful. Having created us, he sees the powerful potential within each of us. Our handicaps and limitations are God given and, therefore, valuable tools in whatever God decides to do, whenever God decides to do it.

God is in the business of developing and working through people. That's why he placed the Holy Spirit in the life of every Christian. So often our tendency is to think only about the things God does through the strengths and abilities of the powerful—heads of state, celebrities, intellectuals, elected officials, international ambassadors. But soak with this thought: God can perform miracles with anybody, and he usually does it through what we perceive to be our handicaps or limitations. He does it through the things we would believe to be insignificant or even unusable. Let these incredible words soak into the fibers of your mind:

9

> Isn't it obvious that God deliberately chose men and women that the culture overlooks and exploits and abuses, chose these "nobodies" to expose the hollow pretensions of the "somebodies"? Everything that we have—right thinking and right living, a clean slate and a fresh start—comes from God by way of Jesus Christ. (I Corinthians I:27, *The Message*)

God is leading us into awesome opportunities!

Far too many of us continue to think that we aren't good at anything, that our inadequacies are so bountiful that God can achieve absolutely nothing through us. Not true! You are a product of the creative hand of God. You are designed the way you are because God thought it was best for you and the achievement of his will. Honor your design—including your limitations—with a spirit of humility.

Develop an Attitude of Satisfaction

I have learned how to get along happily whether I have much or little.
PHILIPPIANS 4:11

We wish we could drive the ball like Tiger Woods or John Daly, play the long irons like Fred Couples or Greg Norman, finesse the short game like Phil Michelson or Lee Trevino, and putt like Dave Stockton Sr. or Brad Faxon. But while regular instruction from a teaching pro and more frequent play would certainly improve our games, we know we'll never match the achievements of these superstars. We'll never become scratch golfers. On average, we will shoot about ten or twelve over par.

That's us! God gifted us to do other things a whole lot better than play golf. Without sounding egotistical, we'd like to think that when it comes to delivering sermons, we shoot par! That's how God made us. And he wired us that way for a purpose. The big question then is this: Are we satisfied with how God made us? Far too many of us exert a great deal of energy wishing and trying to become somebody or something we are not.

Pastor Rick Warren tells a story about an impressionable young boy who said, "Ever since I was little

I never wanted to be me. I always wanted to be Billy Wettington. But Billy Wettington didn't even like me. But I walked and I talked like Billy Wettington. We chose to go to the same school. But that's when Billy Wettington changed. He began to hang around Herbie Vandamen. He walked like him and talked like him. That really messed me up. I began to walk and talk like Billy Wettington who walked and talked like Herbie Vandamen. Then it dawned on me that Herbie Vandamen walked and talked like Joey Haverlan, who walked and talked like Corky Sabenson. So here I am walking and talking like Billy Wettington's imitation of Herbie Vandamen's version of Joey Haverlan's impression of Corky Sabenson. And you know who Corky Sabenson was walking like? Of all people, that dork Kenny Wellington! And that little pest walks and talks like me!"

The Bible says in 2 Corinthians 10:12 that it is unwise, even stupid, for us to compare ourselves with other people. There is absolutely nothing to be gained in that exercise. The happiest people in life are those who recognize who they are, get a firm grasp on their abilities, choose carefully the places for those abilities to be exercised, and play out their lives within them. They never try to become somebody else. They refuse to live fictitious, inauthentic, unrealistic lives.

Unfortunately, most people still spend their lives comparing themselves to other people and, as a result, perceive themselves as insignificant. They are convinced that who they are and what they do well are unimportant.

If you suffer with a sense of insignificance, listen to what the Bible says: "Now there are different kinds of spiritual gifts, but it is the same Holy Spirit who is the source of them all. There are different kinds of service in the church, but it is the same Lord we are serving. There are different ways God works in our lives, but it is the same God who does the work through all of us" (1 Corinthians 12:4-6).

When we recognize our limitations, honor their presence within us, develop and use them as God intended, the church (God's redemptive community on earth) will flourish, and we will find ourselves with a strong attitude of satisfaction.

12

Continue to Be Persistent

Every day you don't hit balls is one day longer it takes you to get better.

Ben Hogan

All of us face moments in our lives when we feel as if nothing is working. That's certainly true with golfers. We all go through periods when we simply don't play well. Our swing has no tempo, we don't feel comfortable over the ball, we struggle trying to read the speed on our putts, or we have no feel with the putter. Serious golfers will try everything they can think of to fix a problem. They will change instructors, tinker with their stance and swing, alter their preshot routine, rearrange their diet, purchase new clubs, adjust the feel of the clubs with weighted tape, even go to a chiropractor. But what they don't do is give up! They stay with the game. They play through difficulties. They are persistent with their work habits until they fix whatever is wrong.

A few years ago Masters champion Ben Crenshaw was having trouble keeping his golf balls on the fairway. Things had gotten so bad that, as he said, "I went fishing the other day and missed the lake with my first cast." We all can point to some major times in our lives when we've felt like that—as if we're in a forty-acre field walking through some tall weeds. And that is a mighty lonely feeling! The challenge in such circumstances is to remain persistent.

I (Gary) went through about a five-month period a decade or so ago when I felt lost. I had always maintained a strong vision of where our church needed to go, when it needed to go there, and what steps we needed to take to get us there. But during that five-month period, my leadership gift seemed gone. I didn't know what steps to take next. I began to think that maybe my leadership role with the church was coming to an end, that maybe the church had outgrown me and my abilities.

Then between Christmas and New Year's Day I wrote a lengthy document about our ministry. It took an entire day. When it was finished, I put it into the hands of the staff and elders and left on a twelve-day missions trip to Nigeria. During the trip there was lots of time for prayer and reflection without the stressful obligations that go with being in the

13

office every day. Several pieces of a plan began to fall into place as my mind worked over the details. By the time I returned home, my vision for the church had been restored. The document I wrote became the catalyst for a fresh mission statement, opening doors of growth for the church. I had continued to play with my God-given handicap—and God rewarded my persistent efforts. "God blesses the people who patiently endure testing. Afterward they will receive the crown of life that God has promised to those who love him" (James 1:12).

Play to Your Strengths

God has given each of us the ability to do certain things well.
ROMANS 12:6 (TLB)

14

Few golfers perform well with every part of the game. For instance, Hale Irwin isn't very long off the tee, but he's a great iron player. John Daly is tremendously long off the tee and has a pretty good touch with the putter, but the short irons give him trouble. Brad Faxon is not overly strong from tee to green, but he's deadly with the putter.

A good golfer capitalizes on his strengths and seeks to manage his weaknesses. If he hits the life out of a four iron, he's tempted to drive with it, chip with it, putt with it—even brush his teeth with it. His confidence is so strong with that club he tends to reach for it every time.

There's a lesson here for living the Christian life. If you are gifted to serve and encourage others, do it! If you are good at teaching, leading, giving, showing mercy and comfort, extending hospitality, providing wisdom and counsel, do it! Do it regularly, do it persistently, do it courageously, do it by faith, do it to honor God, but do it!

God gives us opportunities to use our strengths, but sometimes we don't recognize them because we're so focused on our handicaps. Remember the reference to Moses? When God asked him to serve, to go and lead the effort to free the Israelites from bondage, Moses balked because he didn't think he had the gifts to do it—despite the fact that he had lived in Egypt for many years and understood the culture, the political system, the economic system, even the people he'd be up against. He had spent forty years in the middle of nowhere, undergoing an intense period of preparation before God called him. All Moses could see was his weakness, what he couldn't do well. But God finally convinced him to play to his strengths and then promised him that he would help him work through the weaknesses. God said, "Now go, and do as I have told you. I will help you speak well, and I will tell you what to say" (Exodus 4:12).

That's God's promise to us. In the midst of trials and tough times in life, God promises to help us accomplish amazing and extraordinary things, things we never thought possible. So play to your strengths! Stop focusing on the weaknesses—just let God help you manage them.

If you haven't discovered and accepted your limitations, you won't play within them. You won't play

15

to your strengths, and you won't experience much success. Instead, you're likely to experience a lot of burnout and anxiety—and will soon be tempted to quit. You'll find it hard to be persistent.

Charlie Boswell knew his handicap. He recognized his limitations and learned to play well within them. And he played to his strengths.

Charlie lost his eyesight during World War II while rescuing his friend from a tank that was under fire. He had been a great athlete before his accident, and in a testimony to his talent and determination, he decided to try a brand-new sport, a sport he had never imagined playing even with his eyesight—*golf!*

Through determination and a deep love for the game, Charlie became the National Blind Golf Champion. He won that honor thirteen times. One of his heroes was the great golfer Ben Hogan, so it truly was an honor for Charlie to win the Ben Hogan award in 1958. Upon meeting Ben, Charlie was awestruck and said that he had one wish—to play one round of golf with the great champion. Ben replied that playing a round together would be an honor for him as well, because he had heard about all of Charlie's accomplishments and truly admired his skills. Then followed this conversation:

"Would you like to play for money, Mr. Hogan?" Charlie blurted out.

"I can't play for money—it wouldn't be fair!" said Ben.

"Aw, come on, Mr. Hogan, $1,000 per hole!"

"I can't. What would people think of me, taking

16

advantage of you and your circumstance?" replied the sighted golfer.

"Chicken, Mr. Hogan?"

"OK," blurted a frustrated Ben, "but I am going to play my best!"

"I wouldn't expect anything else," said the confident Charlie.

"You're on, Mr. Boswell! You name the time and the place!"

A very self-assured Charlie Boswell responded, "Ten o'clock—tonight!"

Listen to words of the apostle Paul again, this time with greater meaning: "I was given the gift of a handicap to keep me in constant touch with my limitations. . . . At first I didn't think of it as a gift, and begged God to remove it. [But God said] . . . 'My strength comes into its own in your weakness'" (2 Corinthians 12:7, *The Message*).

Here's the challenge: Recognize and maximize your limitations. Honor God, and be satisfied with what he's given you. Doing so will enable you to press on, play to your strengths, experience fewer bogies—and see more of the pars and birdies God has planned for you. And who knows—you may even get a shot at a hole in one.

17

Golf is in essence a simple game.
Where the average man goes wrong is
in making the game difficult for himself.

P. G. Wodehouse, author

CHAPTER

2

Simplifying Your Game:

STICKING TO THE FUNDAMENTALS

Don't look for shortcuts to God.

MATTHEW 7:13

(The Message)

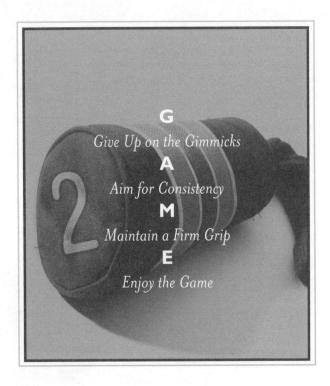

G
Give Up on the Gimmicks

A
Aim for Consistency

M
Maintain a Firm Grip

E
Enjoy the Game

olf boils down to this: hitting a ball from one spot to another, using the fewest possible strokes. But the game has become so technical that it almost requires a Ph.D. in physics to understand it. We suspect that the thousands of instructional books, videos, teachers, and television programs that explain the ins and outs of golf—in laborious detail—have added to the confusion and complexity of the game. Golfer Peter Thomson apparently thinks so. When asked why he had never written a book on golf, he replied, "If I wrote one, it would consist of two sentences. 'Take the club straight back. Then swing it straight through.'"

There is an excellent parallel between what's happened in the game of golf and what often happens in the lives of Christian people. We have a tendency to complicate the Christian life to the point that we lose sight of its essence. We cloud its simplicity and power. We lose sight of its purpose and core values.

When Jesus came to earth, he stepped into a religious environment that was deeply burdened by unnecessary intricacy. In the midst of all that, Jesus was asked, What's most important? What's fundamental to living a life of faith with God? Jesus had a simple answer: "Love God and love people!" (see Matthew 22:37, 39).

In other words, living the Christian life doesn't have to be that complicated. All we need to do is stick to the fundamentals. Here's how:

Give Up on the Gimmicks

I know how easy it is, in the search for self-improvement, to sacrifice fundamentals for gimmicks. . . . When golfing badly, it's easy to suffer the irresistible urge to reach for a Band-Aid remedy.

Jack Nicklaus

We've been noticing ads in the paper about some new golf balls that travel farther than anything on the market. The only problem is, the United States Golf

Association says that they are illegal. If they weren't, everybody would have them—including the pros.

It's tempting to reach for the gimmicks—the Band-Aid remedies—both on the golf course and in life. That irresistible urge presents itself most strongly when we are going through the difficult moments that define our faith. In those moments and throughout life, we have to watch carefully for the cheap substitutions, presenting themselves as genuine elements of growth. Because our needs are often deeply pressing, it's easy to get fooled. We need to pray for a discerning eye to quickly distinguish the gimmicks from the authentic article.

Ephesians 4:14 (TLB) tells us that we should not be like children in our spiritual lives, "forever changing our minds about what we believe because someone . . . has cleverly lied to us and made the lie sound like the truth."

22

Often, spiritual gimmicks sound a lot like the truth. For example, you may have heard this promise offered to people in financial trouble: *If you give a "seed offering" to the Lord, he will multiply it and give it back to you in waves of prosperity, because God didn't intend for Christians to be poor.* There's a skin of truth in that promise. God does honor faith and generous giving. But he also calls for wise stewardship of resources, which involves good financial planning, frugal spending, faithful saving, careful investing, and so forth. To allow ourselves to be captured by glib promises is to give in to gimmicks rather than to seek the fullness of the truth.

One area in which we are especially susceptible to gimmicks: prayer. In the Sermon on the Mount (Matthew 6:7), Jesus warned against babbling on and on when we pray. And yet, so many churches and Christians take the model prayer Jesus gave right after this warning and *repeat it* . . . over and over. Prayer should be a personal conversation with our heavenly Father, but we have a tendency to recite memorized prayers someone else wrote or poetic thoughts we learned as a child. Even in our efforts at learning to pray, we need to be careful about placing too much confidence in formulas that may be helpful as models, but deadly when used as shortcuts to God.

Matthew 7:13-14 (*The Message*) says, "Don't look for shortcuts to God. The market is flooded with surefire, easygoing formulas for a successful life that can be practiced in your spare time. Don't fall for that stuff, even though crowds of people do. The way of life—to God!—is vigorous and requires total attention."

23

Spiritual growth, surviving life's tough challenges, enduring hardships, and enjoying the fullness of God's values in life are never achieved through gimmicks. They come from knowing and sticking to the truth.

Aim for Consistency

The hard, unglamorous reality is that you play well because your swing is built on a solid foundation. When a pro has problems, it's usually because his basics slip.
Tom Watson

Nothing simplifies your golf game like being consistent with the fundamentals, as one of the guys on our staff (we'll withhold his name because we like him) learned recently. To be kind, we need to tell you that he's a novice to the game. (To put it another way—uh—he's not good.) Coming up the eighteenth fairway while playing the other day, his approach shot to the green was slightly less than a hundred yards. He stood over the ball, club in hand, with every intention of putting it softly onto the green. However, succumbing to poor fundamentals, he proceeded to swing at the ball seven times before he actually hit it! Seven straight times he whiffed it badly, allowing his head to shoot up and his feet to pull away with the power of his swing, causing him to pirouette like a ballerina.

24

On the eighth try, firm with the fundamentals, he swung. His shot landed on the green a few short feet from the cup. He was ecstatic! "Oh yeah! Look at that shot!" After nearly falling out of the golf cart with laughter, I (Ken) said, "One out of eight isn't bad." If our friend wants to get better at golf, he needs to repeat the fundamentals until they become a consistent part of his game.

We all struggle with inconsistency—on and off the golf course. One of the greatest obstacles to achieving consistency is trying too hard to look perfect. A favorite phrase of ours is "It's not how well you play, it's how good you look when you show up at the course." In other words, we can fool people about our game by looking like somebody we're not! The problem is, the more time we spend trying to look good, the less time we're going to spend on really improving. The same is true in our spiritual life. As Oswald Chambers said, "Most of us are not consistent spiritually because we are more concerned about being consistent externally."

The Bible is clear that consistency in our spiritual life doesn't come from merely looking good. We can't fake it. Jesus said, "Be especially careful when you are trying to be good so that you don't make a performance out of it. It might be good theater, but the God who made you won't be applauding" (Matthew 6:1, *The Message*).

Another obstacle to achieving consistency is confusing it with perfection. As George Will said, "The pursuit of perfection often impedes improvement. "Never confuse the call to be consistent with being perfect. They are far from the same. Being consistent on the golf course means practicing the fundamentals. In the Christian life, it means regularly thinking godly thoughts, doing godly things, holding godly values, and seeking godly perspectives. Being perfect means making no mistakes. Human beings are not capable of perfection, because only God is perfect. But while we can't achieve perfection, we can make progress—and one of the important measuring rods for progress is consistency.

25

Maintain a Firm Grip
Work on the fundamentals constantly.
Nick Price

The goal in golf is to put that little ball in the cup using the fewest number of strokes from tee to green. We do that best when we practice certain fundamentals: keeping the right grip on the club, positioning ourselves correctly in addressing the ball, using the right hip and shoulder turn when swinging the club, keeping our head down until the club strikes the ball, and finishing the swing with belt buckle pointed toward the target position. That's it!

The goal of the Christian life, as we pointed out at the top of this chapter, is to love God and love people. We do that best when we have a firm G.R.I.P. on four fundamentals:

G

Grasp God's Word

R

Recognize Your Identity

I

Interact through Prayer

P

Practice Obedience

GRASP GOD'S WORD

The Bible needs to be the first thing we reach for when processing the challenges and opportunities of each day. While few of us can quote it at the drop of a hat, we should have a firm grasp on the Bible's principles. Psalm 119:9 (*The Message*) says, "How can a young person live a clean life? By carefully reading the map of [God's] Word."

We should know the principles of God's Word so well that every time we're tempted to do wrong, the teaching of God goes off in our mind like an alarm, warning us to wake up and take appropriate action. We love the words of Colossians 3:16: "Let the words of Christ . . . live in your hearts and make you wise."

Reading God's Word should be a natural and routine part of our lives. Its teaching must touch every part of who we are—every thought, every habit, every idea, every choice, every challenge, every decision, every dilemma, and every activity. No part of us should be off-limits.

RECOGNIZE YOUR IDENTITY

We struggle with being consistent spiritual in our lives because we don't know who we are in Christ. We don't know what's available to us in Christ. But the Bible has already told us what our identity is:

> What marvelous love the Father has extended to us! Just look at it—we're called children of God! That's who we really are. But that's also why the world doesn't recognize us or take us seriously, because it has no idea who he is or what he's up to. But friends, that's exactly

who we are: children of God. (1 John 3:1-2, *The Message*)

What this means is that those who become Christians become new persons. They are not the same anymore, for the old life is gone. A new life has begun! (2 Corinthians 5:17)

But you belong to God, my dear children. You have already won your fight. (1 John 4:4)

We are children of God, new persons, members of God's family. Achieving and living a life that's pleasing and honorable to God is possible through the power that is available to us from the Holy Spirit.

28

INTERACT THROUGH PRAYER

Of all the things the disciples saw Jesus do, the one thing they wanted him to teach them was how to pray. Perhaps it was because they saw that prayer makes things happen. Prayer made things happen before Christ came to earth, and today prayer makes things happen. Exodus 32 tells the story of how the Israelites turned from God and worshiped a golden calf. God had made up his mind to destroy them, but Moses pleaded with him to spare his people. Moses' prayer was effective. God listened. He still listens. James 5:16 (TLB) says, "The earnest prayer of a righteous person has great power and wonderful results." Then there's 1 Thessalonians 5:17-18 (*The Message*): "Pray all the time; thank God no matter what happens. This is the way God wants you who belong to Christ Jesus to live."

What is prayer? Author and pastor Chuck Swindoll may have described it best when he said, "Prayer is realistic, spontaneous, down-to-earth communication with the living Lord that results in a relief of personal anxiety and a calm assurance that our God is in full control of our circumstances."

With that definition in mind, let us get blunt for a moment: Stop worrying about whether you are saying the right words when you pray. Stop fretting over whether you are embarrassed. Stop agonizing about whether or not you remembered everything you should pray for. Stop comparing yourself to other people. Just pray! Pray often! Pray long or short! Stand up or sit down! Do it with someone else or alone! Just do it! Because prayer opens the door for God to work. It leads us to be more spiritually in tune with what he wants for us and from us.

PRACTICE OBEDIENCE

We humans are good at hearing but not very good at doing. James 1:22 (TLB) says, "And remember, it is a message to obey, not just to listen to. So don't fool yourselves." We're also better at talking then doing. As the saying goes, "When all is said and done, there will be more said than done."

We are often asked why we use so many different versions of the Bible when we speak. We say it is because we want to use the version that makes the point clearer than any other. When it comes to Bible translations, the best one is the one you translate into your life, the one that leads to obedience. Far too many Christians believe that the greatest test of spiritual maturity is knowledge. Not true! The real test is character, and character comes from being found faithful in obedience.

When it comes to reading God's Word, it doesn't matter whether you read a chapter at a time or a book at a time, whether you do it every day or every other day, whether you pick morning or evening. Just do it.

When it comes to prayer, it doesn't matter whether you use a list or not, open your eyes or close them, pray silently or out loud, do it morning or night or in between. Just do it.

30

When it comes to obedience, quit worrying about making a mistake. Give it your best shot every day, and let God's grace help you with times of failure.

Enjoy the Game

I am convinced that life is 10 percent what happens to me and 90 percent how I respond to it.
Chuck Swindoll

Most golfers are convinced that if they play better, they will enjoy the game more. We don't disagree with that, but we have sometimes found the reverse to be true too. When we allow ourselves to enjoy the game more, we're less tense and more fluid in our swing, which allows us to play better.

Can the same be said of our spiritual lives? We believe that when Jesus said he came to bring us abundant life, he meant we were to enjoy it. Even through the valleys and shadows, the struggles and hardships, life can be enjoyed. How does one enjoy life—really enjoy it? The answer is probably not what you are thinking. Augustine once answered it this way: "Love God, and do whatever you please."

Most of us think that's not possible. God wouldn't grant such license. People would take advantage of it and stop being faithful. But a biblical understanding of the phrase "love God" is key here. Someone who really loves God would never seek to do anything, or ask anything, or take anything, or think anything that wasn't consistent with who God is and what God teaches. "Take delight in the Lord, and he will give you your heart's desires" (Psalm 37:4).

If we delight ourselves in the Lord, we immerse ourselves, complete ourselves, and fulfill ourselves with everything that is important to him. Therefore, we would only desire to do that which is pleasing to him. And in the end, that which pleases him will more than please us.

Life can be so enjoyable when lived from that perspective.

31

My golf game reminds me of
Woody Hayes's football game—three
yards and a cloud of dust.

Bill Dooley, football coach
Wake Forest University

CHAPTER

Repairing Your Divots:

RESTORING BROKEN RELATIONSHIPS

If you . . . remember that a friend has
something against you . . . go and
apologize and be reconciled to him.
MATTHEW 5:23-24 (TLB)

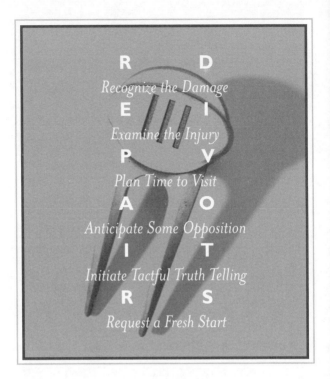

R **Recognize the Damage** D

E **Examine the Injury** I

P **Plan Time to Visit** V

A **Anticipate Some Opposition** O

I **Initiate Tactful Truth Telling** T

R **Request a Fresh Start** S

When you love the game of golf, you're tempted to play it as often as possible—even when you're not on the golf course. Several years ago when my (Gary's) son, Darrin, was still in high school and learning to play the game, we would often find him swinging his clubs in the house. I came home one evening and found a big black mark on the ceiling of the living room. Since he was the only one home, I asked him how it got there. He was reluctant to say at first but finally admitted that it was the result of the tee shot he was trying to hit from the living room into the kitchen. I think he pulled it into the hallway rough!

Darrin's errant tee shot created a "divot" in our ceiling. On the golf course, of course, a divot is a bit different from the black mark in our living room. When a golfer strikes the golf ball, the club continues through the arch of the swing, cutting a piece of sod from the ground where the ball was resting. While the ball heads in the direction of the green (at least that's the intended direction), the nugget of sod flies a short distance, leaving a hole in the ground—a divot. Another type of damage—a ball mark—is created when a golf ball comes flying onto the green and strikes with significant velocity, leaving a small crater. Repairing that ball mark is a top priority for any golfer. Left unattended, a ball mark requires at least fifteen days to repair itself. But when given immediate attention, the damage can be repaired in one day.

It is a golfer's responsibility to replace or repair divots. In our part of the country, the Midwest, that process is completed when the piece of sod is returned to the spot from which it was taken and firmly stamped in place. In other parts of the country, where the soil conditions are different, the golfer is supplied with a container filled with sand, soil, and grass seed to use in repairing divots.

Taking a divot is part and parcel to golf—it can't always be avoided. In some cases, it's even necessary in order to play the game well. But repairing divots is tremendously important to good course care, and it expresses a sensitivity to those playing the game behind you. There is an important spiritual lesson to be drawn here about repairing the divots of life—broken relationships.

Human beings need each other and want to be around each other. You don't have to be a student of the Bible to comprehend that truth. Be that as it may, relationships are not easily developed or maintained. Sometimes it's a struggle. As the film mogul Samuel Goldwyn once said, "Ninety percent of the art of living consists of getting along with people you cannot understand." Somebody else summed it up well: "Life would be great if it weren't for people."

36

The Bible is crystal clear about our need for each other. As difficult as they may be to establish and maintain, the friendships and relationships we establish and cultivate over the years are part of what makes life enjoyable.

When asked, What's the greatest commandment? Jesus said, " 'Love the Lord your God with all your heart, soul, and mind.' This is the first and greatest commandment. The second most important is similar: 'Love your neighbor as much as you love yourself' " (Matthew 22:37-39, TLB). Solomon said, "It's better to have a partner than go it alone. . . . By yourself you are unprotected. With a friend you can face the worst" (Ecclesiastes 4:9, 12, *The Message*). But because of our sinful nature—that motivating force inside of us that often leads us to act in self-centered and deceitful ways—we periodically hurt the people we love.

When, by our actions or words, we've taken a divot from a relationship, we have a responsibility to repair it. God doesn't want us to let injured or broken relationships go unattended any more than we want other golfers to walk on by their divots on the golf course. Repairing both divots and fractured relationships requires immediate attention.

So, what can we do? What should we do? Let us suggest six steps involved in repairing divots and restoring broken relationships.

Recognize the Damage

One of the hardest things in the world to face is our own ignorance.
Source unknown

Over the years, we've observed that an alarming number of golfers create but do not repair the divots they take. Why? In some cases it's because the offendrs are novices. They simply don't know that taking a divot on the golf course or creating a ball mark on the green can significantly damage the playing area. Furthermore, they are so new to the game they don't know the rules or responsibilities. They don't know they're supposed to fix what they tear up.

Ignorance keeps a lot of people from doing what they should—on and off the golf course. When you stop to think about it, few things are as damaging as ignorance in action!

Some people, of course, know what they are doing, but they're too self-centered or inconsiderate
to care. They don't perceive that the damage they
caused is all that important. "What does it matter?
Who cares? If it needs fixing, the maintenance people will take care of it," they say. They're so enam-
ored with their game or in such a hurry to catch up
with their playing partners that they deliberately
choose to disregard doing the right thing. These
people are completely insensitive to the fact that the
damage they created will have lasting consequences
for those coming after them.

On the golf course some of us hook to the left,
and some of us slice to the right, but most of us are
self-centered. How clearly this parallels human relationships. Many people cause damage in their relationships without recognizing it. They float from
one friendship or relationship to another, unaware
of—or deliberately disregarding—the problems they
create. They assume that people are unfriendly to
them or disinterested in them or unwilling to be-
friend them because of fickleness. In reality, however, they themselves are the problem. They may be
ignorant about how to develop and maintain good
relationships. Or they're so self-involved that
they're inconsiderate of the needs of others, so others shy away from them. They're like the man described in Proverbs 18:1 (TLB): "The selfish man
quarrels against every sound principle of conduct by
demanding his own way."

Here's the challenge: Learn to look for the damage you may be causing—on the golf course and in your relationships.

Examine the Injury

Investigate my life, O God, find out everything about me; cross-examine and test me, get a clear picture of what I'm about; see for yourself whether I've done anything wrong—then guide me on the road to eternal life.

PSALM 139:23–24 *(The Message)*

Hitting a ball from a divot is one of the toughest shots in golf. The late Payne Stewart faced that very shot while in the lead at the 1998 U.S. Open championship. It cost him the lead, and he watched Lee Jansen walk away with the trophy.

As Payne Stewart was reminded very painfully in that tournament, the consequences of unrepaired divots can be significant. Divots can leave the golf course vulnerable to disease, weeds, and undesirable vegetation—which can inhibit the flight or roll of a golf ball. Unrepaired ball marks on the green can cause the grass to die. When a green is heavily damaged, it can take an entire season—and a large volume of dollars—to restore it. In the meantime, players are very unhappy if they walk to their ball and find it resting in what seems like a crater the size of the Grand Canyon. This is especially true for serious golfers who play a ball where it lies—or those in tournament play in which the ball is not allowed to be touched between shots. Fortunately, when on the green, a player can mark his ball and repair any ball

39

marks, especially those in the path his ball is intended to take toward the cup. But if a ball mark is several days old, damage may have been done to the point that there are lingering consequences, not only for players but also for course managers and owners.

Can you see how the concepts we've just discussed transfer from golf to the relationships we all have? Far too often we pay little or no attention to the lingering consequences of injuries we've caused. Divots of unkind words can leave gaping holes in the recipient's self-esteem. Divots of selfishness can create broken relationships, as one of our friends discovered the hard way. Having suffered through several difficult relational problems, he decided he wanted to have more "me time," as he put it. Looking back several years later, he said, "I took so much 'me time' that I woke up one day and realized I didn't have any friends!"

Divots of dishonesty break down trust, alienating us from each other. How unstable life becomes when we can no longer trust our friends—even worse when we lose trust in a family member or spouse. Each day's existence is guarded with barriers raised for protection. Fellowship and fun are limited. Conversations that explore opportunities, dissect problems, or seek counsel on deeply sensitive areas are replaced with superficial words. The long-term by-products of these circumstances can be relational seclusion, divorce, fractured families, substance abuse, emotional—or even physical—trauma.

As advanced as our culture is these days, you would think that we would have a real edge on resolving human conflict—that we'd be doing a better job than past generations in creating long-lasting relationships. But our observation is that we are doing a poorer job rather than a better one. We need to start examining the injuries that we are causing in our relationships—and we need to ask for God's intervention. We need to say to him, along with the writer of Psalms: "Investigate my life, O God, find out everything about me; cross-examine and test me, get a clear picture of what I'm about; see for yourself whether I've done anything wrong—then guide me on the road to eternal life" (Psalm 139:23–24, *The Message*).

41

Plan Time to Visit

Confess your sins to each other and pray for each other so that you can live together whole and healed.
JAMES 5:16 *(The Message)*

Repairing a divot on a golf course requires attention, time, and effort. It's something that can't be done long-distance. And generally speaking, the same is true for a divot in a relationship. Broken relationships often require a face-to-face visit—a visit in which meaningful conversation takes place that includes explanation, understanding, caregiving, and agreement.

Too many modern relationships are broken and then left unrepaired. Ironically, a contributing factor is often technology, the same technology designed to give us more free time to build better relationships. We have our computers complete with voice mail, E-mail, fax, CD-ROM, and video, all of which soak up time and attention. We often have several televisions in our home, and family members scatter to watch their favorite shows. Or, because we each enjoy a different style of music, we retreat to one of the CD systems around the house. While all these things can speed up the distribution of information, they diminish genuine communication and eliminate the look-each-other-straight-in-the-eye, feel-the-words-you-hear kind of interaction that is necessary for good conflict resolution.

42

Take a look at your relationships. How are you dealing with the divots of conflict and disagreement? The Bible speaks very directly to our responsibility whenever relationship chaos and conflict tear up our friendships. Matthew 18:15 (*The Message*) says, "If a fellow believer hurts you, go and tell him—work it out between the two of you. If he listens, you've made a friend."

A divot-repairing visit is something done privately, just between you and the other person involved. It should be approached gently. Don't attack by using words that question or demean the other person's character. Instead, say something like, "I know you never intended to hurt me, but the fact is I am hurt. I have some things I'd like to talk about if you'll let me." Through this approach you can set the stage for nonthreatening conversation.

It often takes a planned visit to repair a divot—or a broken relationship.

Anticipate Some Opposition
You have to expect a little detour now and then.
Greg Norman

If a guy is having a bad round with lots of errant shots and his playing partners offer instruction or advice, he's likely to be pretty snarly with his response. So it is when it comes to sitting down and having a heart-to-heart talk with someone you've hurt or offended. If the divot in the relationship is good sized or if there is more than one and they've been left unattended for some time, you can anticipate some opposition when you approach the conversation. Just because 43 you've made up your mind that you need to talk with the other person, made all the arrangements to do it (right place, right time, even the right way), you can't assume that he or she will respond cordially. Solomon knew how it could be: "It is harder to win back the friendship of an offended brother than to capture a fortified city. His anger shuts you out like iron bars" (Proverbs 18:19, TLB).

So, what should our response be when we meet opposition? What we usually do is bite back! We snap and crackle in response to the other person's response, don't we? But the Bible tells us the right way to deal with the negative responses of others. 1 Peter 3:9 says, "Don't repay evil for evil. Don't retaliate when people say unkind things about you.

Instead, pay them back with a blessing. That is what God wants you to do, and he will bless you for it."

How often have you attempted a conversation with someone who responded negatively and you dealt with it by using sarcasm? Peter tells us to respond to a negative comment with a blessing. Then there's Romans 14:1 (*The Message*): "Welcome with open arms fellow believers who don't see things the way you do. And don't jump all over them every time they do or say something you don't agree with."

That's great advice, but it takes a mature perspective to follow through with it. Remember: Periodic opposition is to be expected. Allow the Holy Spirit help you respond in a godly way.

44
Initiate Tactful Truth Telling

Say only what is good and helpful to those you are talking to.
EPHESIANS 4:29 (TLB)

Have you ever golfed with a weekend hacker who expects to perform like a PGA professional—and reacts with uncontrolled anger when he doesn't? You know the person we're talking about—the guy who throws a club when he hooks a shot into the forest or follows every missed putt with a stream of words that would make a sailor blush.

We recall golfing with a friend, who shall remain nameless so as to save our friendship, who suddenly slammed his putter into the ground and took a huge chunk out of the green. None of us said anything that day—perhaps we were too shocked—but we should have. When we allow behavior like that to continue without comment, it not only creates a big divot, but we end up carrying an extra club in our bag called a relational wedge. And a relational wedge often causes a broken relationship.

The key to restoring broken relationships is learning how to be a tactful truth teller. The Bible is clear about this issue. Zechariah 8:16 (TLB) says, "Tell the truth. Be fair. Live at peace with everyone."

Greg Norman nailed the first step in becoming a tactful truth teller when he said, "If you're serious about improving your play, be brutally honest with yourself." Learning to be a truth teller begins with self-examination. Ask yourself, "Am I in the habit of being up-front—factual, pertinent, and to the point—with other people? Or do I prefer to keep the peace by avoiding confrontation at all costs?"

Taking the avoidance approach means you'll never express—or deal with—the truth. Your conversations, and therefore your relationships, will always be superficial and shallow.

When we begin to be honest with ourselves we may discover that we aren't being very truthful with others. And if that's the case, it's no wonder that we are dissatisfied with our relationships, short on friends, unfulfilled in marriage, and outside the loop with our children.

So take a look inside. Are there some old divots that need attention? Like your spouse did something without checking with you and it really hurt

45

your feelings, but you've been hiding your emotions—for several days or weeks? Or there's a job evaluation you've been asked to write and some serious mistakes that need to be documented and discussed, but you are afraid of the stress your truthfulness might cause—so you've been delinquent in finishing it? Or perhaps your child has been involved in something you don't approve of and it needs to be addressed, but you are afraid of the reaction you're going to get and what might be required from you by way of discipline—so you've let it pass? Ephesians 4:15 (TLB) reminds us, "Lovingly follow the truth at all times. . . ."

We need to get beyond our harmful relational patterns and discover ways to be transparent with each other. Failure to do so will cause our relationships to deteriorate into distrust and bitterness at worst or shallow superficiality at best.

If you'd like to initiate tactful truth telling in your life but don't know how, consider this: You have to start somewhere. Pick one negative event, one hurt feeling, one misunderstood word, and resolve to bring the conflict out into the open.

Be prepared for the possibility that following this advice may make you feel miserable at first. We remember seeing a sign that read, "You will know the truth, but it will make you miserable." The initial discomfort you feel at risking confrontation may cause you to think that life would be easier if you just kept denying the truth and bypassing all the tough steps it takes to reveal it. But your misery will be short-lived. The cleansing on the other side, the feeling of relief, the joy of having cast a heavy burden aside will be significant. Count on it. Jesus said, "You will know the truth, and the truth will set you free" (John 8:32).

James 1:19-20 adds one more dimension to this issue: "Dear friends, be quick to listen, slow to speak, and slow to get angry. Your anger can never make things right in God's sight." In other words, restoring broken relationships requires that we be truth hearers as well as truth tellers. Don't you love it when people say, "Do you want the truth—or should I lie to you and make you feel good?" If we want to tell the truth in our relationships, we must be willing to hear and receive the truth when it is expressed to us. Proverbs 12:1 says, "To learn, you must love discipline; it is stupid to hate correction."

Relational divots cannot be restored without dealing with the truth—and then taking one more important step that will provide new opportunities for growth and restoration.

Request a Fresh Start

The pat on the back, the arm around the shoulder, the praise for what was done right, and the sympathetic nod for what wasn't are as much a part of life as golf itself.

Former president Gerald Ford

For a golfer who's having a bad day, who can't seem to get the elements of his or her game together, expressions of care and concern speak of starting over, making a fresh start.

Resolving conflict brings repair to the emotional divots in our relationships. It restores whatever brokenness we have experienced.

Three difficult but necessary phrases help bring about the fresh start we all desire.

PHRASE #1—I WAS WRONG!

Without practice, this phrase tends to get caught in our throat. It's the ultimate in truth telling, requiring an enormous amount of humility. But the wisdom of Proverbs 28:13 (TLB) motivates us to say it: "A man who refuses to admit his mistakes can never be successful. But if he confesses and forsakes them, he gets another chance."

PHRASE #2—FORGIVE ME!

There can be no fresh start without forgiveness. "If you . . . remember that a friend has something against you . . . go and apologize and be reconciled to him" Matthew 5:23-24 (TLB). Of course, when others need your forgiveness, you should follow the advice in 2 Corinthians 2:7-8 (TLB), "Now it is time to forgive him and comfort him. Otherwise he may become so bitter and discouraged that he won't be able to recover. Please show him now that you still do love him very much."

48

PHRASE #3—I NEED YOUR HELP!

We can't resolve relationship problems alone. We can make efforts toward it and seek to be at peace as far as it depends on us, but the cooperation of the other person is required if full restoration is to take place. It's a humble act, a selfless move, but it's absolutely necessary.

These three phrases, offered sincerely and given the appropriate amount of time to sink in, should conclude with a fresh start.

One thing you can count on in golf and in life is this: You will undoubtedly take a series of divots. Divots are inevitable, but destruction is optional. As you look back over your life, do you see any unrepaired divots? Do you see the broken pieces in your relationships? Whether they were on hole two, six, ten, or eighteen—it's never too late to try to repair them.

49

Of all life's pursuits, golf is least susceptible to perfection. We are going to make mistakes.

Kevin Nelson, author

CHAPTER

Using Your Mulligan:

GETTING SECOND CHANCES

For surely you have a wonderful future ahead of you. There is hope for you yet!

PROVERBS 23:18 (TLB)

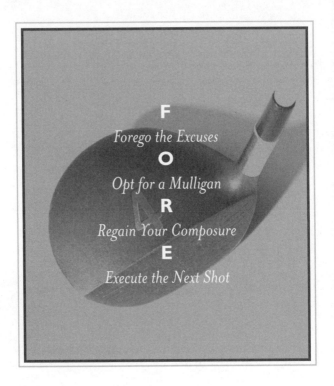

F *Forego the Excuses*

O *Opt for a Mulligan*

R *Regain Your Composure*

E *Execute the Next Shot*

Golf is a hard game to figure," Bob Hope once said. "One day you'll go out and slice it and shank it, hit all the traps and miss every green. The next day you go out, and for no reason at all, you really stink."

That brings to mind a story. Several years ago, three friends and I (Gary) made a commitment to play at least one round of golf together each year. That's not very often for good friends, but because we are all busy pastors living in different states, getting together isn't easy.

One February, the four of us—Bob, Joe, Dudley, and I—met at Disney World to soak up some Florida sun and, of course, play golf. Joe made a tee time for us at the Osprey Ridge course, which has a stunning layout designed by Tom Fazio, that winds through dense vegetation and rolling terrain. Anticipating a great day with old friends, we made our way to the course, paid the fees, and approached the first tee with great expectations.

Now, you need to know that Bob and I have a long-standing rivalry. Neither of us wants to lose to the other. This particular day, our round began quite evenly, but as we neared the end of the front nine, Bob pulled ahead. By the time we reached the turn, I knew I needed to step up my game or I'd be razzed all week about who won. After taking a break for some hot dogs and soda, we tackled the back nine. My game got slightly better, but Bob's fell apart—too many hot dogs, no doubt! Intending to regain the lead he had just lost, Bob teed up his ball on the sixteenth hole, looked down the fairway and started his backswing with a strong hip and shoulder turn. But as he pulled the club through the shot, he turned it over and duck-hooked a low line drive into the woods. A huge mistake! With a sheepish look on his face, he walked to the back of the tee and asked, "Am I the worst golfer you've ever played with?"

His voice was so pathetic that I laughed until I nearly cried. When I regained my composure I asked, "Would you like to hit it again?" I was offering him a second chance or, as it's known in golf, a mulligan.

Anybody who plays golf with some regularity knows what a mulligan is—it's the privilege playing partners offer each other to hit another shot without penalty, an opportunity to correct a mistake without having to deal with the consequences on your scorecard. As James Dyet points out in *Out of the Rough,* a mulligan is "a product of sheer, undeserved kindness. It can't be earned; it can only be received. It's golf's grace gift!"

Although not officially allowed in golf, playing partners will often agree to allow each other one mulligan per nine holes. That way, they can step up to the first tee knowing that even if they top a shot, hook it into the trees, slice it into the water, or miss it altogether, they'll get a second chance.

54

What an interesting concept—a second chance! When it comes to bad shots in life, are there any second chances? When we find ourselves in the midst of a moral foul-up, when we've made a huge mistake in judgment, when we've overlooked the most important value in our lives, is there a second chance? Is there someone in authority who will say, "Use your mulligan"? You bet there is! God offers us a second chance—that's what his grace is all about. Through the person of Jesus Christ, all of our sin is forgiven, and life can begin again. Fresh! New! Guilt-free! Every part of our sordid past, every terrible mistake, every addiction, every wrong thought is wiped from the record. "What happiness for those whose guilt has been forgiven! What joy when sins are covered over! What relief for those who have confessed their sins and God has cleared their record" (Psalm 32:1, TLB).

Both mulligans and grace are about starting over, about second chances. To obtain a second chance—in golf and in life—consider these F.O.R.E. things:

Forego the Excuses

A man who refuses to admit his mistakes can never be successful.
PROVERBS 28:13 (TLB)

Picture this all-too-common scenario: A golfer walks to the first tee, tees the ball up, looks down the fairway in the general direction he intends to hit the ball and then goes through his personal preshot routine. He draws the club back and powers through the shot—only to watch the ball dribble off the tee or squirt left or right, creating an embarrassing moment. Then come the excuses:

- *The ball was teed too low.*
- *I can never hit with this driver.*
- *My back is so stiff.*
- *I knew I needed a new golf glove.*
- *I just can't rotate well on my left side.*
- *I had a feeling it might not be my day.*

Most of us like to pretend that our game is better than it actually is, so we make excuses for our poor play. It makes no sense, because none of us should expect to play perfect golf. Even golf legend Walter Hagen once said, "I've never played a perfect eighteen holes. There is no such thing. I expect to make at least seven mistakes a round."

As in the game of golf, we tend to make excuses for our mistakes in life. Few of us like to say, "I blew it today. I failed. I messed up big time. I really sinned!" But the Bible says that without confession, there is no second chance. If we are unwilling to confess, God continues to track the penalties on his score card; we force him to apply the rules. 1 John 1:8 says, "If we say we have no sin, we are only fooling ourselves and refusing to accept the truth." But the good news comes in the next sentence (verse 9): "But if we confess our sin to him, he is faithful and just to forgive us and to cleanse us from every wrong."

One note: Confession shouldn't be selective, like that of the taxpayer who wrote to the IRS: "Gentlemen: Enclosed you will find a check for $150. I cheated on my income tax return last year and have not been able to sleep ever since. If I still have trouble sleeping, I will send you the rest." We need to be confessing daily, completely, humbly, and in detail.

Confessing our sins—foregoing our excuses for wrong behavior and admitting to our shortcomings—opens the door to a second chance.

Opt for a Mulligan

I don't know where I would be without the mulligan. OK, I confess—I do know. I'd be thirty feet off the tee box or in deep rough or out of bounds or in a water hazard or behind the ball washer.

James Dyet, Out of the Rough

We were playing golf together on the Illinois State University course when we came to the eighth tee, which has a tricky dogleg right. Ken teed up his ball and hit a towering shot right on the green—unfortunately, right on the green of the *seventh* hole. He was so overjoyed at the opportunity to take a mulligan that he proceeded to hit the ball to the seventh green two more times. Gary thought that was hysterically funny, but the guys on the seventh green weren't too happy.

Chi Chi Rodriguez once said, "The sweetest two words are 'next time.' " When it comes to our sin and failure, we all hope for a "next time," don't we? Well, here is some good news: The Bible is full of examples of people God worked with and used despite their failures.

57

- *Abraham was called the friend of God, though he had once been an idol worshiper.*
- *Moses became a great leader who delivered God's people out of slavery, despite the fact that he once committed murder.*
- *Jonah became a Billy Graham to the Ninevites, even though he had tried to walk away from God.*
- *David became a "man after God's own heart," although he had seduced his neighbor and killed her husband so he could marry her.*
- *Peter was the first person to proclaim the full message of the gospel after Jesus' resurrection—but sixty days earlier he had denied Christ.*
- *Paul wrote thirteen books in the New Testament, although he had once been a terrorist against the church.*

We all need mulligans—let's admit it! So what does God do that enables us to opt for a second chance? To receive forgiveness and start over? Just listen:

> He has not punished us for all our sins, nor does he deal with us as we deserve. For his unfailing love toward those who fear him is as great as the height of the heavens above the earth. He has removed our rebellious act as far away from us as the east is from the west. (Psalm 103:10-12)
>
> Once again you will have compassion on us. You will trample our sins under your feet and throw them in the depths of the ocean. (Micah 7:19)
>
> And I will forgive their wickedness and will never again remember their sins. (Jeremiah 31:34)

It's as if God writes our names on an Etch-a-Sketch along with all the terrible habits we are unable to shake, the lies and deception, the addiction that's getting worse, the growing practice of sexual fantasy. And then, after we genuinely confess, he shakes it, and the sins are gone in an instant. Furthermore, they can't be retrieved!

After he committed adultery, King David came face-to-face with God—and learned that he was a God of second chances, that he offered mulligans. Listen to David's response once he learned this truth: "But you forgive! What an awesome thing this is" (Psalm 130:4, TLB).

A footnote: God's grace is always balanced with truth—with a call to begin taking his teaching on holy living seriously. In other words, we must be extremely careful not to develop the mind-set portrayed by comedian Emo Phillips: "I used to pray every day for God to bring me a bicycle," he said. "But then I figured out that God in his infinite wisdom doesn't work that way. So I just stole one and asked him to forgive me."

It's all too easy to take the attitude, *It doesn't matter what I do, because God loves me. God is in the business of forgiving people, right?* But Romans 6:1-2 says, "Should we keep on sinning so that God can show us more and more kindness and forgiveness? Of course not! Since we have died to sin, how can we continue to live in it?"

It would make no sense to hit a bad shot just so we can use a mulligan. The whole purpose of a second chance is to move from disaster to success, from penalty to prosperity. If we deliberately break up our marriage, lie on the job, mistreat our neighbors, break promises, take liberties we know we don't deserve—and then justify our actions by calling on God to forgive us and grant us another chance—we've abused God's grace. We've attempted to manipulate him based on our own selfish desires. Jude 1:4 warns us against people who try to convince us that we can do just as we like without fear of God's punishment. And 1 Peter 2:16 (TLB) says, "You are

59

free from the law, but that doesn't mean you are free to do wrong. Live as those who are free to do only God's will at all times."

God is your playing partner in life. If you want a second chance, let him know you want to opt for a mulligan.

Regain Your Composure

Nobody wants to win more than I do. But if I give it my best shot and fail, then life goes on.

Jack Nicklaus

A few years back, John Daly and Fuzzy Zoeller, two of golf's most colorful personalities, were playing eighteen of golf's toughest holes on eighteen different golf courses as part of a made-for-television event. Standing on the eighteenth tee at Pebble Beach, John hit a horrible shot and started to throw his club. Fuzzy interrupted him and said, "Let me help you." He then took John's titanium driver and threw it into the Pacific Ocean. Fortunately, they both laughed. Golf can be very frustrating, but life goes on.

In both golf and in life, we cannot move on if we remain tied to failure. Getting a second chance is all about getting better and doing better. Recently a woman called me (Gary), asking some heavy questions and wanting some answers. She was wrestling with deep inner turmoil over losing her husband through a divorce. I tried to provide some biblical teaching and perspective to her situation, assuming that her loss was a recent development. But when she related the chronology of her circumstances, I found that her anger and hurt had been festering for years. She was paralyzed. She couldn't move on with her life because she couldn't regain her composure. Listen to what the Bible says in Isaiah 43:18-19: "But forget all that—it is nothing compared to what I am going to do. For I am about to do a brand-new thing. See, I have already begun! Do you not see it?" Unfortunately, this woman did not see it.

Regardless of our expertise at golf, we all hit bad shots now and then—we even string several of them together before recovering. No matter where we are on the maturity scale, we all experience moments of sin and failure: a lack of judgment, a slip of the tongue, a bad choice, an inappropriate thought or attitude. Those of us who are serious about life express disappointment with ourselves when these things happen, but after receiving God's forgiveness, we have to regain our composure if we want to move forward with joy. Hebrews 12:1 (TLB) says, "Let us strip off anything that slows us down or holds us back, and especially those sins that wrap themselves so tightly around our feet and trip us up."

Execute the Next Shot
Think ahead. Golf is a next-shot game.
Billy Casper, professional golfer

Getting ready to hit that tee shot again may be just the confidence builder you need to shoot your ca-

61

reer best, to advance your golf game in a way you've only dreamed up until now. So disregard whatever happened earlier. Stop reliving your embarrassment over your last shot. Stop thinking about what you did wrong. It's over. Done. Finished. It's time to start thinking about all the opportunities you have to do things right. Bobby Jones, named one of the fifty greatest athletes in the twentieth century (ESPN's *SportsCentury*) had the right idea when he said, "It's nothing new or original to say that golf is played one stroke at a time. But it took me many years to realize it."

Spiritually speaking, once God grants forgiveness and provides you with a second chance, every day becomes an opportunity for a whole new adventure. There are new challenges, new goals, new perspectives. Just because you've made one mistake (or a golf bag full of them), life is not over. God doesn't want you to be bogged down by the poor choices of the past. He wants you to be hopeful about the future. He is! Life is lived one hopeful day at a time. "For surely you have a wonderful future ahead of you. There is hope for you yet!" (Proverbs 23:18, TLB)

So next time you find yourself ready to put away the clubs or give up on life, remember God's wonderful promise: "But these things I plan won't happen right away. Slowly, steadily, surely, the time approaches when the vision will be fulfilled. If it seems slow, do not despair, for these things will surely come to pass. Just be patient! They will not be overdue a single day!" (Habakkuk 2:3, TLB)

You may want to hang that verse on your golf bag or on the mirror of your bathroom—along with this phrase from Chuck Swindoll: "It's never too late to start doing the right thing."

Alas, the world is still a testy par five.
Jim Murray, sportswriter

CHAPTER

Avoiding the Hazards:
OVERCOMING LIFE'S OBSTACLES

Friends, when life gets really difficult,
don't jump to the conclusion that
God isn't on the job.
1 PETER 4:12
(The Message)

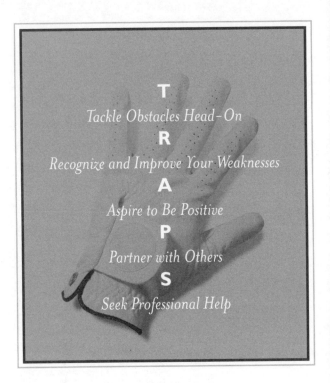

T — Tackle Obstacles Head-On

R — Recognize and Improve Your Weaknesses

A — Aspire to Be Positive

P — Partner with Others

S — Seek Professional Help

rustrating as they can be, hazards on the golf course have some upsides: They force golfers to play smart, to be alert, to manage the game strategically—and to restrain the temptation to pull the clubs from the bag and "grip 'em and rip 'em."

Sometimes the hazards on the course are unplanned. Take what happened at the Rancho Palos Verdes Golf Course in southern California, for example. After a landslide completely ripped the eighteenth green off its foundation, the green came to rest on an ocean bluff below, creating not only a treacherous new hazard, but an especially difficult 1,300-yard par five.

Obstacles are everywhere, both on the golf course and in our spiritual journey! Some obstacles in the Christian life can't be avoided, but most can—especially those involving sin. What's required is a careful outlook, a sharp spiritual mind, and the keen work of the Holy Spirit.

The Bible exhorts us to stay out of the way of certain obstacles. Proverbs, for example, teaches us to watch out for the wicked traps that might trip us up: "If you keep your mouth shut, you will stay out of trouble" (Proverbs 21:23). "Above all else, guard your heart, for it affects everything you do" (Proverbs 4:23).

67

But what are we supposed to do about unavoidable obstacles? What would you do, for instance, if you were faced with circumstances like those that confronted Dallas and Sharon Davis? Their daughter Kathy was one of 168 innocent people killed in the bombing of the Federal Building in Oklahoma City. In the two years that followed, the Davises lost another daughter to lung cancer and a son to an automobile accident.

For most of us, tragedies like these would be huge obstacles to peace of mind and faith in a loving God. But here's something we need to remember in the middle of adversity: "Friends, when life gets really difficult, don't jump to the conclusion that God isn't on the job" (1 Peter 4:12, *The Message*).

And yet, isn't it our natural tendency to feel like maybe God isn't doing his job, that he's out to lunch at the exact moment we need him? When life's obstacles obliterate our happiness, we are often left asking questions like the one posed in the movie, *Oh, God, Book II,* in which a young girl asks God (portrayed by George Burns), "Why do you let bad things happen?" God responds, "There can't be good without bad, life without death, pleasure without pain. That's how it is. If I take sad away, happy has to go with it."

Here's what Jesus had to say about the hazards of life: "In this godless world you will continue to experience difficulties. But take heart! I've conquered the world" (John 16:33, *The Message*).

Can you imagine a golf course without hazards? No sand traps, no water, no tricky greens or gusty winds. No trees or waste bunkers. No rainstorms, divots, ball marks, downhill putts, or thick rough? That wouldn't be a golf course—it would be a football field with holes in it. Though you want to avoid them at all cost, hazards point up the beauty of the playing area. They help players develop their skills, plan ahead, and proceed with discipline.

On or off the golf course, troubles are a distinct possibility. Some we can and should stay clear of. Others we may need to recover from after having been temporarily ensnared. All call for us to move through life on guard and alert to the fact that difficulties come into play regularly.

What can we do about life's hazards? Here are five good steps we can take:

Tackle Obstacles Head-On

There are two things keeping me out here. Faith in God and faith in myself. I'll never quit.

Bobby Clampett, professional golfer

Golfers have no choice but to tackle hazards head-on—unless they decide to cheat. Some players have been known to employ techniques like foot mashies (kicking the ball) and hand wedges out of the sand bunkers (throwing the ball). While such cheating does indeed give relief from the hazard, it doesn't offer the satisfaction of conquering the obstacle through skillful play. It's simply avoidance.

In the normal course of life, we can't avoid obstacles by pretending they don't exist. But many people try. We know people who, because they are in major financial bunkers, never open the mail because it might contain bills. They just throw it away—out of sight, out of mind. We've also known people with major health problems who chose not to go to a doctor. Still others have avoided facing issues from their childhood that stem from a dysfunctional relationship with their parents. It's tempting to ignore the hazards of life, but God's counsel is straightforward on this matter: "Don't try to squirm out of your problems" (James 1:4, TLB). Why? "God blesses the people who patiently endure testing. Afterward they will receive the crown of life that God has promised to those who love him" (James 1:12).

We will never overcome life's obstacles by avoiding them. If we want to live fulfilled, contented lives, we must tackle hazards head-on, seeking counsel and praying for wisdom as we do.

Recognize and Improve Your Weaknesses

If you could improve your weaknesses, you would improve your game. The irony is that most people prefer to practice their strengths.

Harvey Penick, golf instructor

Ever go to a practice range? What are most people doing there? They're on the tee with a driver and a bucket of balls, seeing how far and hard they can hit. This is curious given that 60 percent of golf is played inside of one hundred yards. And 40 percent of the game is putting! But nobody wants to practice that part of the game. What's more, nobody wants to rehearse hitting out of the hazards—pitching out of the sand bunkers, wading through long grass swales, chipping downhill, or fishing a ball out of the pond. We all like the power of driving the golf ball off the tee.

Did you ever hear the old story about the golfer who trained a gorilla to play golf? This gorilla could hit 400-yard drives. When people saw the gorilla in action they were utterly amazed. After watching him hit an astounding drive one day, a golfer standing nearby said, "How does he putt?" The owner replied, "The same way he drives."

This story hits close to home for me (Ken). On a weekend trip to Hilton Head Island in South Carolina I was enjoying the Eagle's Pointe Golf

Course, which was designed by Davis Love III. I hit several 300-yard drives on par-four holes no longer than 350 yards. But I scored a six every time! It was so bad that I earned the nickname "The Sheik" because of my apparent affinity for the sand traps. Serious golfers know: *Drive for show, putt for dough. It's not how you drive, it's how you arrive.* But because I'm pretty good at driving, I'm tempted to neglect my short game.

Most of us tend to bring a golfer's mentality to our spiritual lives. In other words, if we are gifted in music, we have no trouble volunteering to sing in the choir. If we are gifted to teach, we quickly take on a children's class, lead a growth group, or conduct a seminar on child rearing or marriage. If we are gifted with mercy, we are the first to be there for people in trouble, aiding the discouraged, guiding the misdirected, comforting the bereaved. But what are we doing in the areas where there are known weaknesses in our lives? What are we doing about our lack of wisdom, our lack of spiritual discernment, our sporadic prayer, our inadequate Bible knowledge, or our proclivity to certain unhealthy habits? In other words, what are we doing about the things that often lead us into hazards?

If we only spend time doing the things we are good at—or the things we enjoy—life will be out of balance. We'll be targets for all the hazards. If we don't work on changing our bad habits and tendency to sin, we will repeat them. The Bible urges us to improve: "You used to do them when your life

71

was still part of this world. But now is the time to get rid of anger, rage, malicious behavior, slander, and dirty language" (Colossians 3:7-8).

One of the best strategies we have for dealing with obstacles is to improve on the weaknesses that lead us to them.

Aspire to Be Positive

Is your life full of difficulties and temptations? Then be happy, for when the way is rough, your patience has a chance to grow.
JAMES 1:2-3, TLB

Golfers know the destructive nature of a negative attitude on the golf course. Few golfers improve their play by losing their temper all the time, cursing the course layout each time they play, throwing their clubs when they miss-hit a shot, or kicking their golf bag.

So it is when we try to overcome the obstacles that come our way in life. Sometimes these obstacles are big. Sometimes they're our fault because our weaknesses have gotten out of hand. Sometimes they just happen because the ball of life bounced that way. However or how often they block our way, we can choose to approach them with either a negative or positive attitude.

This story quoted in the *Bible Illustrator* helps make the point: A young college student had two problems common to many students: low grades and no money. She needed to communicate both problems to her parents, but she knew they would have trouble

72

understanding. After considerable thought she wrote this creative letter:

> Dear Mom and Dad,
>
> Just thought I'd drop you a note to clue you in on my plans. I've fallen in love with a guy named Jim. He quit high school after grade eleven to get married. About a year ago he got a divorce. We've been going steady for two months and plan to get married in the fall. Until then, I've decided to move into his apartment (I think I might be pregnant). At any rate, I dropped out of school last week, although I'd like to finish college sometime in the future.

73

On the next page, she continued:

> Mom and Dad,
>
> I just want you to know that everything I've written so far in this letter is false. NONE of it is true. But Mom and Dad, it IS true that I got a C in French and flunked math. It IS true that I'm going to need some more money for my tuition payments.

Even bad news can sound like good news if it is seen from a certain vantage point.

So much in life depends on our attitude as we face difficult circumstances. Remember these important words: "I'd say you'll do your best by filling your minds and meditating on . . . the best, not the worst; the beautiful, not the ugly; thing to praise, not things to curse" (Philippians 4:8, *The Message*). If we want to overcome life's obstacles, we need to maintain a good attitude.

Frank Wren was general manager of the Baltimore Orioles baseball club. After some questionable trades and free-agent signings, rumors began to circulate that he could lose his job. His troubles soon hit close to home. His eight-year-old twin boys were being taunted by classmates who teased them by saying, "Your dad's going to be fired." When Wren learned of the jibes, he told his kids, "Don't worry, because if I get fired, that means I get to stay home and play with you every day." That was good enough for Colby and Kyle, who started jumping up and down chanting, "Fired! Fired! Fired!"

Sometimes all it takes is a different perspective to turn things around.

Partner with Others

During four hours of golf, partners blend their skills, battle the course, and bond their souls. When the final putt sinks and the scores are tallied, they remember the best shots and excuse the worst. Then, after a hot dog and a can of pop, they go their separate ways, and each is better prepared for the challenges he must face alone.

James Dyet, Out of the Rough

One of the great things about golf is that even though you play *for* yourself, you don't have to play *by* yourself. How many business deals have been struck in between golf shots? How many problems resolved? How much money saved? How many visions cast? Questions answered? Dreams shared? In some cases the is actual game gets lost because of the fellowship being enjoyed. A friend said the other day, "Golf is a special relationship. There isn't anything else that I would be willing to do with another person for five straight hours." Golf is a game that is meant to be shared.

The Christian life is meant to be shared as well. Fortunately for us, God never designed it as a solitary existence. Though we sometimes try the solo route, most of us know how much better life is when it is shared with other people, especially those who have a similar vision and values. The Bible is replete with stories of dynamic duos—and we are not talking about Batman and Robin—people who, regardless of their strengths, weaknesses, and varied backgrounds, overcame insurmountable obstacles together: Moses and Aaron, David and Jonathan, Aquila and Priscilla, Paul and Silas, Peter and John.

If you read the biblical stories of what these pairs went through, you will discover how important each partner was to the other. Alone, they would never have achieved the projects God gave them or survived the obstacles they encountered. Instead, they were there for each other, often with encouragement, sometimes with prayer, now and then with correction and warning, periodically with counsel. Through it all they were partners!

So, think about your life for a moment. Who routinely serves as a caddy for you as you walk your way through the hazards life throws in your course? If you don't have such a person, you're likely to position yourself where the obstacles and hazards seem bigger than life itself. You may be dominated by fear—a negative attitude that sees only failure and no success.

What kind of struggles are you facing today? What obstacles are hindering your spiritual growth? What hazards seem to have taken your breath away? Are you attempting to handle them alone? If so, maybe that explains your limited success. Here's the lesson: Find a partner (or more than one), tee it up, and challenge the course together.

Seek Professional Help

Be frank with your pro about what you want from his help, but remember that he is the expert.

Dr. Richard Coop, author

Our PGA teaching professional, Ray Kralis, tells us that many of his students try to tell him how they need to be taught. Instead of opening themselves to instruction, they try to heal their own golf ailments. They don't listen to Ray until they have run out of options. A similar dynamic is at work in life away from the golf course. God is our professional life instructor who knows what is needed to succeed. Unfortunately, the tendency of many people is to call on God only when they hit bottom.

When we do hit bottom, however, it is God we call on. The investor who loses money in the stock market never says, "Wall Street help me." The businessman who loses his job never says, "Corporation help me." The soldier who finds himself crouching in a foxhole in the middle of a war never says, "Government help me." The natural human tendency is to call on God in a crisis. Why is that? Because woven into our mind, body, and spirit is an undeniable inclination to seek God. This proclivity is seen best in moments of crisis. When they are cowering in fear, when they are pushed to the limit, even people who have expressed no faith in the reality of God seem to go to him involuntarily. Entreaties to God—sometimes sounding like profanity—gush from their lips.

77

We all want to overcome the obstacles and crises we face, but we've been rudely awakened to the fact that doing it alone isn't working, and as important as good partners are, it's not enough. The Bible provides a feasible alternative to the ineffective methods of most people today. Listen carefully, "So humble yourselves under the mighty power of God, and in his good time he will honor you. Give all your worries and cares to God, for he cares about what happens to you" (I Peter 5:6-7).

Right now you may feel as if your life is shattered into a million pieces—that it is beyond repair. But, let us tell you some good news. God can do great things with the "ugly rounds" of your life as long as you are willing to seek his help.

Calvin of the Calvin and Hobbes cartoon series once said, "Give me the strength to change what I can, the inability to accept what I can't, and the incapacity to tell the difference." Like Calvin, we may not be able to pray this prayer correctly. However, we need to seek God's help because he knows what we need before we ask him. His full intent is to help us deal with and recover from life's obstacles. Remember these words from Psalm 34:19 (*The Message*): "Disciples so often get into trouble; still God is there every time."

Every golfer has a fault he falls back into repeatedly. The trick is learning what that fault is and how to correct it.

Ken Venturi, golf analyst

CHAPTER

Keeping Your Head Down:

CORRECTING BAD HABITS

You are a slave to whatever controls you.

2 PETER 2:19

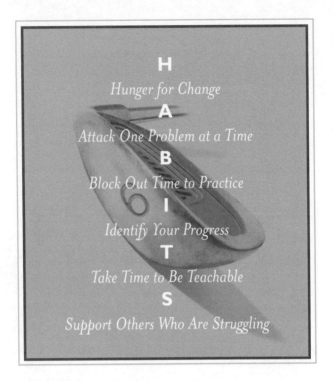

H *Hunger for Change*

A *Attack One Problem at a Time*

B *Block Out Time to Practice*

I *Identify Your Progress*

T *Take Time to Be Teachable*

S *Support Others Who Are Struggling*

Virtually all golfers—even the great ones—struggle with bad habits. During a very difficult round, Lee Trevino once said, "My swing is so bad I look like a caveman killing his lunch."

There are several classic bad habits in golf: breaking your wrists too soon, swinging too high or too low, and, perhaps the most common, lifting your head too soon. This last habit has to do with the fact that many of us like to watch our shot—where it goes, what it does in flight, and what kind of bounce it takes when it hits the ground. So we're compelled to look up before the club strikes the ball, creating an opportunity for all kinds of things to go wrong. We end up topping the ball or pulling off of it—leaving the club head closed at impact and sending the ball sharply left. Or our hips may release too soon—leaving the club face open at impact and sending the ball sharply right.

Bad habits have bad consequences not only on the golf course but also in life. The guy who has a bad habit of not recording his ATM card transactions will face the same dilemma as the person who says, "I can't be out of money—I've still got checks." The cook who has a bad habit of looking away while slicing vegetables is at risk of filleting off a finger. The farmer who has a bad habit of looking at the scenery while plowing—instead of keeping his eye on a point at the end of the field—is going to end up with a row that looks like a dog's hind leg.

This chapter is about minimizing or eliminating those negative little behaviors we all have—about which we say to ourselves in private moments, *I wish I didn't do that. I'd feel better if I didn't do it. Life would be better without it.* We're talking about things like: Overeating. Watching too much television. Overspending the family budget. Using coarse language. Losing our temper. Ignoring key priorities.

Why make a big deal about a couple of a little habits? Because, as 2 Peter 2:19 points out, "You are a slave to whatever controls you."

Bad habits aren't trivial—they can get in the way of spiritual growth and become a significant deterrent to achieving our potential. What's more, bad habits can become addictions, and addictions can destroy people's lives.

If a bad habit has attached itself to you, don't shrug it off. Don't ignore it or allow yourself to be satisfied living with the tarnished parts of who you are. Take a long look at it. Assess what the long-range effects will be if you continue to hang on to it. Work at correcting it before it takes an even more destructive turn in your life.

There are several simple steps that you can use to help you break free of bad habits. Before we tell you what they are, let us emphasize one point: The longer you wait to implement these suggestions, the harder it will get. "Muscle memory" is just as strong with bad habits as it is with good ones. If you recognize that a bad habit is nagging at your life, slowing your production, obstructing your education, or hindering your progress, quit telling yourself that one of these days you are going to change it. Waiting only allows the habit to become more deeply ingrained. Those who are serious about change begin immediately. Those who only talk about it find excuses.

Back to our suggestions—here are some ways to overcome the bad habits that are hindering your progress:

Hunger for Change

We cannot become what we need to be by remaining what we are.

Max DuPree, management consultant

Change—now there's a scary word! It's been said that the only person who likes changes is a wet baby. There's a story of a woman who bought a piece of needlework at a craft fair. These words were stitched on it: *Prayer Changes Things.* Proud of her purchase, she took it home and hung it above the fireplace in the family room. Several days later she noticed it was missing. When she asked her husband if he knew what had happened to it, he said, "Yes, I removed it." Obviously disappointed she asked, "Don't you believe that prayer changes things?" He responded, "Yes, I do. I just don't happen to like change, so I took it down."

Several years ago, I (Gary) was moaning about my terrible putting while playing golf with some friends. Finally someone in my foursome said, "You need a new putter. The one you're using is ancient and doesn't fit you." I was very proud of my admittedly antique putter because it went way back in my family. Playing with it was like driving a classic car, even though I wasn't playing well with it. For a while I couldn't believe that a new putter would make much difference in my game. But my friend's words continued to ring in my ears, and as things turned out, my son gave me a new putter for Christmas. When I used it, I couldn't believe how quickly my game improved. Although I had resisted change, once I submitted to it I improved almost immediately.

Most of us resist change, even when it's good for us—even when it's in our best interest. An example: Have you ever noticed where the most frequently

83

used keys on a typewriter or computer keyboard are located? They're very far apart. The original purpose of this arrangement was to slow down typing speed. Back in the 1800s, typewriter keys would jam if the typist went too fast. Then about 40 years ago, the Dvorak Simplified Keyboard was developed. With this keyboard, the most frequently used keys were all placed on the home row, and the right hand did 56 percent more work than the left. Tests showed that typists could greatly increase their speed—up to five times—with no increase in errors. Still, we labor on keyboards designed to be inefficient. Why? We don't like change.

But if we want to continue to mature in Christ, if we want to get rid of bad habits, change is mandatory!

The moment we embraced a relationship with God, we entered into the process of change. God's plan for us has always involved change. Listen to this: "From the very beginning God decided that those who came to him—and all along he knew who would—should become like his Son" (Romans 8:29, TLB). And then there's this: "Don't become so well-adjusted to your culture that you fit into it without even thinking. Instead, fix your attention on God. You'll be changed from the inside out. . . . Unlike the culture around you, God brings the best out of you, develops well-formed maturity in you" (Romans 12:2, *The Message*).

Ken Blanchard says that there are four distinct levels to real and long-lasting change:

Level #1: Knowledge change. Real change begins with new information. It's the easiest part in the process that leads to change. You change people's knowledge by providing them with new information.

Level #2: Attitude change. The information given begins to change how people feel and think. This is a tough step but necessary. Action never comes before attitude.

Level #3: Behavior change. When the attitude is strong enough it prompts a behavior change. Attitude creates motivation that causes people to want to do something . . . to get rid of one thing and put something else in its place.

Level #4: Organizational change. That's where an entire group changes. It takes three to five years, generally, to make major change in an organization. For instance, it's much easier to start a new church than to change an old one, because it is tough to redirect power.

Think through the first three points of Ken Blanchard's process for change. Apply them to yourself. Isn't it true that you only seek to change what you do when you are provided with *information* that alters your *attitude?* That's true. But it's a good thing! If God has change in mind for all of us from the moment we come to him through Christ (and he does), then it's no wonder he wants us to continue to study his Word and interact with him through prayer. Prayer and study lead us to think like him and ultimately change our behavior to correspond

85

with his. The more we act like him, the less we are
enslaved by bad habits.

The challenge: Hunger for change!

Attack One Problem at a Time

Correct one fault at a time. Concentrate on the one fault
you want to overcome.

Sam Snead

Golf is a complicated game. It encompasses countless
variables that all have to do with hitting the ball: grip,
stance, placement of the ball in the stance (which can
differ with each shot), distance to the ball, posture,
alignment, backswing, hip and shoulder turn, club
speed, follow-through—just to name a few. There
isn't anything easy about golf. Learning to play it and
improving your play involves attacking one piece of
the game at a time. Tony Lema, one of the top three
or four players in the game when he was killed in a
small-plane crash in 1966, emphasized this point
when he said, "You build a golf game like you build a
wall, one brick at a time."

So it is with most other things in life. Whether it's
learning to use new computer software, or learning
to cook, or learning tax laws—to become good at it,
you have to learn one aspect at a time. It's just like
that when it comes to growing in our spiritual lives—
in particular, getting rid of bad habits. We don't
change overnight. We don't get everything right in
one day.

We not only have to deal with bad habits one at a

time, we often have to take the factors that contribute to bad habits and deal with them one at a time. If we're trying to lose weight, for example, we have to remember not to overstock the refrigerator, or leave the Girl Scout cookies out on the counter, or stop at McDonald's every day on the way to work. And we have to give attention to how we think about food. As we're told in Proverbs 4:23, "Above all else, guard your heart, for it affects everything you do."

The spiritual battle is fought in the mind before is fought anywhere else. Whatever captures our attention will capture us. Whatever we spend the most time thinking about is exactly what we will end up doing.

Bad habits aren't changed quickly. Be patient, be diligent, and conquer one thing at a time.

87

Block Out Time to Practice

There is nothing in this game of golf that can't be improved—if you practice.

Patty Berg, professional golfer

We've only found one group of people who likes to practice. It's the adult choir at our church. Here's how we know: twice as many people come to practice during the week as show up to sing at church!

Regardless of the activity or sport, changing bad habits into good ones only happens through good practice. One of the things that made the Chicago Bulls so good through much of the 1990s, in addition to the incredible talent of Michael Jordan, was their work ethic in practice. Players who joined the squad from other NBA teams often commented on it. They couldn't believe how hard the team practiced—especially Michael Jordan, the guy who never looked like he needed to practice.

Any coach will tell you that a team's or individual's game performance will directly correlate to the amount of time and energy expended in practice. Getting rid of our bad habits requires concentrated effort on learning a new skill. It takes repeating the new skill often enough so that when we find ourselves in a pressure situation we won't revert to the old habit.

We used to say "practice makes perfect." This isn't exactly true, because no one is perfect. But practice does make habits, and when we practice good habits until they outweigh bad habits, our conduct will be more right than wrong.

Since conduct follows thought, we must practice having the right thoughts. When we repeat the right thoughts often enough, they will remain, even in the face of temptation or crisis, thereby creating right conduct. Perhaps this is what the apostle Paul was getting at when he wrote the words "Fix your thoughts on what is true and honorable and right" (Philippians 4:8).

A decision to merely stop a bad habit won't work unless it is replaced with new thoughts that stimulate new activities. If that doesn't take place, the old habits will return quickly, and it will be harder than ever to get rid of them thereafter. Bottom line: Getting rid of bad habits requires a lot of practice, concentrating on the right thoughts that create right actions.

Identify Your Progress

Give your complete attention to these matters. Throw yourself into your tasks so that everyone will see your progress.

1 TIMOTHY 4:15

Identifying our progress is a major step in getting rid of bad habits and building new, more positive habits. Success breeds success. Knowing that we're improving encourages us to continue improving.

How can we know we're making progress? It helps if we have some markers, some measures of success. There are a number of possible markers of improvement in golf. A consistently lower score is one. Less fatigue is another. More fairways and greens reached in regulation is still another.

89

When we start striking the ball well, we gain confidence from knowing that our bad habits are being replaced by good, fluid mechanics—and our technical improvement is eventually going to be reflected in our score.

So it is with the habits that plague our spiritual lives. We are able to move forward more consistently when we can see measurable progress—and in order to measure our progress, we need some indicators of success. For example, we can sense progress if we take note of the fact that we're only having two bad thoughts a day as opposed to the six we used to have. We sense progress in changing our eating habits when we weigh ourselves and find that we've lost ten pounds. We sense progress in changing our speaking habits when we realize that it's been four days since anyone has criticized us for using slang. We sense progress in changing our habitual attitudes when we realize that it's been a week since anyone took us to task for our negative thinking.

The Bible gives us some great insight and encouragement about how identified progress can lead to further growth. 2 Peter 1:5-7 says, "So make every effort to apply the benefits of these promises to your life. Then your faith will produce a life of moral excellence. A life of moral excellence leads to knowing God better . . . to self-control . . . to patient endurance . . . to godliness . . . to love for other Christians, and finally you will grow to have genuine love for everyone."

Take Time to Be Teachable

Don't be too proud to take lessons. I'm not.
Jack Nicklaus

The best golfers have a teachable attitude. Like Jack Nicklaus, they continually seek to improve their game. A similar principle applies to people undertaking other endeavors. Whatever the field—computers, accounting, investments, architecture, graphic design, interior decorating, cooking, construction, risk management, agriculture, medicine, law, education—or whatever the sport—tennis, basketball, soccer, football, swimming—staying current and doing well requires constant improvement. Those who don't remain teachable decline in their skills, succumb to bad habits, and cease to be effective.

The same is true of spiritual growth. To grow spiritually, we need to get rid of our bad habits—and getting rid of bad habits requires that we remain teachable. Here is what the Bible says on the subject: "Tune your ears to wisdom, and concentrate on understanding" (Proverbs 2:2). "Listen for God's voice in everything you do" (Proverbs 3:5, *The Message*). "Plans go wrong for lack of advice; many counselors bring success" (Proverbs 15:22). "If you stop listening to instruction, my child, you have turned your back on knowledge" (Proverbs 19:27).

91

After reading those Scriptures about the importance of developing and maintaining a teachable spirit, how would you rank yourself? Very teachable? Somewhat teachable? Occasionally teachable? Seldom teachable? Not very teachable? Thought about being teachable once?

We are not just talking about what you are like when you attend a church service and listen to the message. We are talking about the general pattern of your life every day. We are talking about your attitude toward learning, no matter where the lesson comes from: superior or subordinate, spouse or sibling, friend or foe, celebration or crisis. Success in getting rid of bad habits depends greatly on our willingness to be teachable.

Support Others Who Are Struggling

He comforts us in all our troubles so that we can comfort others.

2 CORINTHIANS 1:4

After playing golf one day with former president Gerald Ford, who's been known to get a bit wild with his shots, Bob Hope said, "Whenever I play with Gerald Ford, I try to make it a foursome—the President, myself, a paramedic, and a faith healer." While poking some fun at the former president's inconsistent play, Hope offers a hint of mercy in his joke—a statement, intentional or otherwise, about the need to extend assistance to those struggling with their game.

One of the things we've noticed about many good players is how often they encourage players who are having difficulty. There's a great lesson here for those of us who have made some progress in moving beyond our bad habits. We're going to encounter those who are still struggling with their habits—who are still looking forward to what we've achieved. When and where appropriate, we need to graciously respond with support—to "offer comfort as we have been comforted."

One of the amazing things about God's plan is this: He wants to take our weaknesses, the things we are ashamed of, the things that embarrass us, things we would like to hide, and turn them around so that we can assist other people. There is something very powerful about a community of people who are willing to do that for each other.

We are convinced that one reason our congregation has grown so rapidly, from 1,500 to 2,700 in a
two-year period, is the fact that as a community, we
have realized we are a bunch of imperfect people
working with each other, under God's leadership
and by his design, to bring positive changes to each
other. We're working on our bad habits—hungering
for change, attacking one problem at a time, block-
ing out time to practice new habits, identifying our
progress, and supporting each other as we struggle.

Maybe it's time to change the way you approach
life. Think about this saying, one that we have found
to be very true: "Insanity is doing the same thing
over and over again expecting different results."
What habits are driving you crazy? Why don't you
pick one right now and commit yourself to working
on it until you achieve the results you desire?

93

CHAPTER

The Mental Game:

DEVELOPING A POSITIVE ATTITUDE

Don't copy the behavior and customs of this world, but let God transform you into a new person by changing the way you think.

ROMANS 12:2

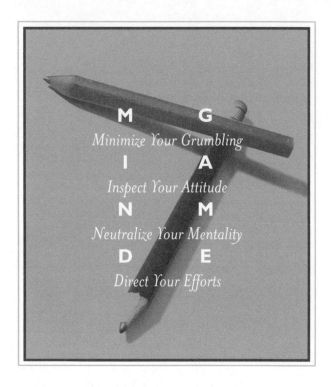

M G
Minimize Your Grumbling
I A
Inspect Your Attitude
N M
Neutralize Your Mentality
D E
Direct Your Efforts

The Pelican Hill Golf Club in Newport Coast, California, designed by Tom Fazio, is a breathtaking masterpiece, named by *Golf Magazine* in 1998 as "one of the top 100 courses you can play." I (Ken) had been looking forward to an opportunity to enjoy the course, where virtually every hole overlooks the ocean, and on a mild, sunny day in May the conditions could not have been more perfect. Jeff, my number-one golfing partner, and I arrived early to capture and enjoy every minute. We wanted to be mentally prepared to beat the mountainside course into submission.

We started well and were having one of our classic "Jack and Arnie"—type battles. I was confident that this would be my day. After all, I wasn't about to let a Midwestern farm boy defeat me on a course in the part of the country where I had grown up. Little did I know that my breakfast would play a significant role in destroying my mental game.

We had purchased some doughnuts—the breakfast of amateurs!—and I was saving mine to eat later in the morning. But something unusual happened on the sixth tee box. While we were on the tee box, two squirrels hijacked our cart, confiscated my bag of doughnuts, and before I could yell, "Fore!" started feasting on my apple fritter! I was shocked! I felt violated! I was hungry! My mind quickly shifted from golf to these glorified gerbil gangsters, who had evidently set up an elaborate crime syndicate in south Orange County. They were all I could think about for the next few holes—and my score reflected it.

97

Later that day I attempted to elicit some pity from the young woman in the beverage cart. But she was not the least bit sympathetic. "Oh yeah!" she said casually. "They steal everything out here. I hope you still have your wallet!"

I figured that if I was paying over $200 for a round of golf, the management should at least provide security guards to protect me from the squirrels. Is this unreasonable? I did manage to get my mind back in the game, though, and I'm proud to say I held on for a one-stroke victory.

Unfortunately, the squirrel incident has scarred my memory of a truly marvelous golf course. It's an example of the kinds of experiences that cause us to focus on the negative things in life, even when everything else is perfect.

How's your mental game? How do you react when things don't go your way?

In a video about his basketball career, Michael Jordan also talked about other parts of his life, such as his growing passion for golf. "The mind comes into this game so much," he said. "It comes into basketball, too, but sometimes your skills can over-come the mind a little bit. But in golf, if your mind's not in it, then you can forget it." Serious golfers know how right Michael is. The game cannot be played well without a positive attitude.

If ever an event threatened to destroy a player's attitude, it was the 1996 Masters golf tournament. Greg Norman entered the final round six shots in the lead, only to have his powerful swing lose its patented accuracy. He had an opportunity to go down in history as one of golf's immortals—and lost it. According to Ed Sherman, sportswriter for the *Chicago Tribune*, "No golfer ever messed up a big lead in a major the way Norman did at the [1996] Masters."

It wasn't the first time Norman had fallen short of winning one of golf's four major championships. He had finished second in seven previous major tournaments—the 1984 U.S. Open, the 1986 Masters, the 1986 PGA, the 1987 Masters, the 1989 British Open, the 1993 PGA, and the 1995 U.S. Open. The 1996 Masters was a chance to prove himself as a champion. What happened to him at that tournament could have blown his confidence so badly that the rest of the tour year would have been ruined. But Greg refused to allow that to happen. His attitude and perspective were right on.

"Losing this Masters is not the end of the world," he said afterward. "I let this one get away, but I still have a pretty good life. I'll wake up tomorrow, still breathing, I hope. All these hiccups I have, they must be for a reason. All this is just a test. I just don't know what the test is yet. I'll win here. I will. Something great is waiting for me down the line in golf. I don't know what it is, but I have to believe that. If I don't, I might as well put my clubs away for good."

99

At the end of the 1996 season Greg Norman was fifth in scoring and fifth all around. He finished fifteenth on the money list at $900,000 and won the Doral Open along the way. And he continues to maintain a positive attitude—good times or bad.

Like Greg Norman, we need to keep a positive attitude—not just to excel at golf, but to develop spiritually. The Bible says that what we think about every day is what we will end up doing. Thought precedes action. What captures our attention captures us. Hear the words of 2 Corinthians 10:5 (*The Message*): "We use our powerful God-tools for . . . fitting every loose thought and emotion and impulse into the structure of life shaped by Christ."

Attitudes are a powerful part of who we are. There are a lot of things that God asks us to do and be, but without the right perspective they cannot be achieved. Furthermore, life doesn't always go as planned. As someone once said, "Life is what happens to you when you're making other plans." We need to ask ourselves what type of attitude we will possess when the stuff we didn't plan for happens.

In June of 1997 my (Gary's) dad was diagnosed with prostate cancer. As he began undergoing the many tests necessary to determine the extent of the cancer and the best prescribed treatment, he said to me, "This is something we wish hadn't happened, but it has and we've accepted it. We know we are in God's hands, we have the best doctors, and we've looked around and found a lot of people far worse off than us . . . so we've decided to maintain a good attitude and handle what comes. . . . as a matter of fact, we are planning to play golf first thing tomorrow."

Some might say that in choosing to have a positive attitude despite his difficult circumstances, my dad was playing a mind game. If so, it's the kind of mind game we all need to play—one that involves four steps:

Minimize Your Grumbling
A bad attitude is worse than a bad swing.
Payne Stewart

100

Payne Stewart was right—a bad attitude *is* worse than a bad swing. Why? Because a bad swing can't be fixed until the attitude is fixed. Life won't be enjoyable until our attitude is right. And the attitude can't be right if we continue to gripe and complain.

Have you ever played with golfers who are always grumbling? They never have enough time to warm up. They don't like the layout or how the greens keeper tends the course. The fairways are too narrow. The greens are too heavily bunkered. The rough has been left too long. Their list of complaints is endless.

The children of Israel had a lot of complaints during their years of hardship in the desert. After years of oppression as slaves to the Egyptians, they had welcomed deliverance under Moses and looked forward to their Promised Land. But did they ever whine and complain when their pilgrimage took them through the desert.

When life takes us through the desert, many of us have a tendency to grumble and blame God. In so doing, we move ourselves farther and farther from his power and grace. We become bitter, angry, hardhearted, ruthless. We drive wedges in relationships. We decrease the size of our circle until we're the only one in it. What a miserable existence.

Philippians 2:14 says, "In everything you do, stay away from complaining." Is there any more difficult command to fulfill?

Inspect Your Attitude

When my attitudes are right, there's no barrier too high, no valley too deep, no dream too extreme, no challenge too great for me.

Chuck Swindoll

We all have attitude—either positive or negative—and life's tough experiences reveal which kind it is. Legendary basketball coach John Wooden once said, "Sports do not build character. They reveal it." The same is true of our attitudes. When life begins to disintegrate, our basic attitudes are quickly revealed.

When a golfer's game takes what appears to be a sudden turn south—he's hit several bad shots in a row, his score is climbing, he's shanked several balls into the water, he's putting like a gorilla—he is often revealed to be either an "excuser" or a "chooser." The excuser can always find a host of reasons why his poor play is not his fault:

- *My back is so stiff.*
- *It's cold, and my hands can't grip the club.*
- *It's hot, and my hands are sweaty, and I can't grip the club.*
- *I knew I needed new clubs.*

Excusers refuse to take responsibility for their lack of practice, poor fundamentals, lazy execution, lack of knowledge or limited concentration. Instead, they transfer blame.

Many of us are tempted to be excusers off the golf course as well as on it. We want to blame our failures and lack of spiritual growth on rotten parents, a lousy job, lack of money, limited education, or a shortage of opportunity. We make excuses for ourselves instead of taking responsibility for our actions and attitudes.

If ever someone had a legitimate excuse for a negative attitude, it was Ken McGarity. At age nineteen, he was horribly wounded in the Vietnam War when his helicopter crashed after being hit by a rocket grenade. His life was saved, however, by Dr. Kenneth Swann, who amputated his legs and supervised surgeries on his eyes, arms, and head. The next day, several of Dr. Swann's colleagues criticized him for his decision to operate, saying McGarity would have been better off dead. For years afterward Dr. Swann was filled with anguish and doubt. Finally, in 1989, he decided to find McGarity. The doctor expected his former patient to be hospitalized but instead found him happily married. He had earned a college degree, learned to scuba dive, and was in the process of earning a second degree in an effort to help others like himself who are without legs and unable to see. Not only was he not bitter at the doctor for saving his life, he was very grateful. "If Dr. Swann hadn't stuck all the pieces back together, I wouldn't have this wonderful wife and these great children," he said.

Ken McGarity made no excuses. He didn't blame or feel sorry for himself. Instead, he chose to maintain a positive attitude. Life is what we choose to make it, depending on our attitude. There are two

103

words in the English language that are very close to-gether—*bitter* and *better*. One letter spells the differ-ence. It's the letter *i*—being *bitter* or *better* is determined by what "I" choose.

Like Ken McGarity, you and I can choose to have a positive attitude. But it won't happen unless we consciously choose to make it happen.

Neutralize Your Mentality

If you want to change yourself, you must change how you think.

Harvey Penick

Choosing to have a positive attitude means we have to neutralize the negative mentality that often plagues us. How do we do that? According to lead-ership consultant John Maxwell, we first need to eliminate certain vocabulary words from our speech:

"I can't . . ."

"I don't think . . ."

"I'm afraid of . . ."

"I don't believe . . ."

"It's impossible . . ."

Conversely, Maxwell says, certain words should become a part of our vocabulary:

"I can . . ."

"I know . . ."

"I am confident . . ."

"I do believe . . ."

"God is able . . ."

104

Author Kevin Nelson said in *The Golfer's Book of Daily Inspiration,* "Instead of 'I can't,' I say 'I can.' Instead of 'I hope,' I say 'I will.' Instead of second-guessing myself, I trust myself. Instead of dwelling on mistakes, I accept them and move ahead. Instead of worrying about what could go wrong, I focus on what I do right. Instead of pondering my weaknesses, I assert my strengths." A good idea for all of us.

We're not suggesting that we artificially portray a new attitude. Instead, we suggest that we can move from being negative to being positive by changing how we think—through the power of God. Romans 12:2 reminds us, "Don't copy the behavior and customs of this world, but let God transform you into a new person by changing the way you think."

If we begin thinking positively, we are in line for a positive attitude.

Direct Your Effort

Keep putting into practice all you learned from me and heard from me and saw me doing, and the God of peace will be with you.
PHILIPPIANS 4:9

The good thoughts that you've been thinking as a result of the inward change God has been producing in you are now ready to be placed into practice. Good actions follow good thoughts. In fact, good actions are produced by good thoughts.

In a lengthy interview following his disastrous performance at the 1996 Masters golf tournament,

Greg Norman was asked what he had learned, if anything. He responded that he had gained a deeper respect for the compassion of people, which had made him less critical of the public. He reported that people's response to him after that tournament was like a big security blanket affirming him as a person. For example, he said: "A man came up to me during my son's football practice and said, 'I've been meaning to write you, but now I'm glad I didn't because I can tell you to your face. What you did at the Masters and how you handled it has changed my life and the way I handle things.'"

Greg said he thought, "Here, I'd lost a tournament and yet changed someone's life." As a result, he said, "I think I'm a little easier, a little more appreciative. Bottom line, it has probably changed my life more than winning the Masters would have."

That's the influence of a positive attitude. Don't settle for anything less. And remember, keep an eye out for those squirrels!

It's not how fast you get there,
but how long you stay.

Patty Berg

CHAPTER 8

The Back Nine:

FINISHING STRONG

*Caleb said, "Today I am eighty-five years
old! I am as strong now as I was when Moses
sent me on that journey, and I can still travel
and fight as well as I could then."*

JOSHUA 14:10-11

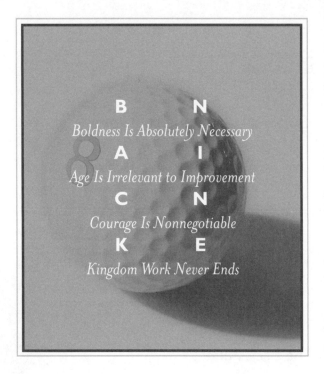

B
Boldness Is Absolutely Necessary

N

A
Age Is Irrelevant to Improvement

I

C
Courage Is Nonnegotiable

N

K

E
Kingdom Work Never Ends

One of my (Ken's) most unusual golf experiences happened on a warm summer day at one of the oldest courses in St. Louis. Called Forest Park, it literally weaves in and out of a city park.

Golfing that day was an adventure that gave a whole new meaning to the phrase "avoiding the hazards." People were rollerblading on the cart paths, and families were picnicking on the fairways! While I was teeing off on one of the par-three holes, two women casually strolled barefoot across the green. The course ranger periodically used a megaphone to warn people about watching for flying golf balls.

These people didn't belong on the golf course—certainly not during play—but there they were. My partners and I couldn't escape the commotion, which was extremely distracting, and our concentration was completely broken. As a result, our front-nine scores were atrocious. I will refrain from revealing the exact numbers, but let's just say that if your mutual funds climbed that many points in one day, you'd be very wealthy!

Determined not to let ourselves get discouraged, we chose to continue playing. I rallied my playing partners with a phrase that I now use anytime my score on the front nine begins with the number four or higher: "All right, guys, it's time to regroup and get ready for the back-nine championship."

I am happy to say that I turned things around that hot day in St. Louis and won the "back-nine championship" on one of the weirdest golf courses I've ever played. Having been distracted at the beginning of the course, I was able to finish strong.

In golf, finishing strong means playing our best on the back nine despite distractions or failure earlier in the game. In the Christian life, finishing strong means keeping our eyes focused on the Lord—and our goal—throughout the cycles of life.

Our definition of the "back nine" of Christian living depends on our stage of life. For some of us, the back nine is about growing older. It feels like it happened so quickly. In the blink of an eye, we go straight from pimples to wrinkles. Many people find it hard to continue growing spiritually when they get older. It's illogical, but the older we get and the longer we are Christians, the more susceptible we are to giving up or sitting down.

For others, the back nine of the Christian life has to do with difficult circumstances and past defeats—heartaches, mistakes, wrong assumptions, and poor choices that damage our self-esteem, frighten us, hurt our feelings, and make us feel like a failure. Spiritual growth seems way out of reach, virtually untouchable. As a result, too many times, we quit!

For still others, the back nine of Christian living takes the form of overwhelming responsibilities. Having two or three children back-to-back will consume a parent's attention and energy for long periods of time. The demands of children are immense, and those early childhood days offer few breaks. Young parents don't intentionally isolate themselves from the Christian friends and activities that used to bring them together in fellowship. They don't intend to neglect their spiritual development, but their heavy load of parental responsibilities often convinces them that they have no choice.

For those in the back nine of later life, the temptation is to say, "I've served my time. Let the younger people have their turn." By that, we usually mean that we want the younger people to provide the human resources for demanding projects, but we—because we are older, wiser, and have more experience—want to continue our role as the decision makers. We are more than willing to give up the rigors of active involvement, just not the reins.

For those in the back nine of difficult circumstances, the temptation is to say, "I am too embarrassed and hurt to continue. God isn't interested in failures, and I'm the biggest of them all." We may want to continue on and finish strong, but negative voices have convinced us that there is no hope.

Several years ago a commercial captured the attention of the entire nation. Do you remember it? An elderly woman is lying on the floor of her home, and she yells out, "I've fallen and I can't get up!" Perhaps this commercial drew so much attention because so many of us can relate to it. We know what it means to stumble through life. We've made choices that have left us wondering if we'll be able to get up and try again.

For those of us who feel growing responsibilities converging on us like the stifling humidity on an Illinois golf course in the middle of August, there's often an overwhelming urge to give up the game. Thinking that they are doing the right thing, those with pressing demands may put off serving in the church and or actively seeking to grow in Christ, intending to start again at a later date. Often, later never comes.

The temptation to give up, to quit, or to put off hits people at different times. For some, it strikes when they have children or when they step out of adolescence. For others, it's when they experience the empty-nest syndrome. For still others, it's when they reach retirement. Whenever it occurs, it isn't healthy. Experience on the golf course tells us that some of the greatest plays, some of the best shots made, some of the finest moments are captured on the back nine.

In what areas of your life do you need to finish strong? Career? Marriage? Child rearing? Staying healthy? Maintaining spiritual disciplines in your walk with Christ?

One of the best role models we know of for finishing strong is Caleb, whose story is found in Joshua 14:6-13. If Caleb's life were depicted on the AMC channel, it would quickly become a movie classic. Caleb would be to finishing strong what John Wayne is to westerns, Arnold Schwarzeneggger is to action films, Jerry Lewis is to comedies, and Vincent Price is to horror films.

Caleb's life story comes to the forefront of biblical history shortly after the children of Israel crossed the Red Sea following their deliverance from bondage in Egypt. They were headed for the land of Canaan, located in what today are Israel, Lebanon, and the occupied territory. Before the Israelites invaded the land promised to them by God, they sent twelve spies to check it out. Ten of those spies returned with fear in their eyes, terrified of what they saw, and absolutely convinced that taking that piece of real estate would be an impossible task.

Joshua and Caleb saw things differently. Their perspective was spiritual, not human. At the ripe age of forty, Caleb saw life through the eyes of an almighty, sovereign God. He knew that all things were possible through the Lord! Caleb never doubted. He was convinced to the marrow of his bones that with God all things are reachable.

Tragically, the Israelites chose to listen to the report of the other ten spies. And since they chose not to believe God, they wandered around in the desert another forty years. Only Caleb and Joshua survived that purifying period. Everyone else died. A new generation of people with new spiritual values finally moved forward and occupied the very land God had promised. At eighty-five years of age, Caleb (along with Joshua) was still leading them. Despite forty years of setbacks, he was finishing strong.

113

Caleb's story offers us several principles for finishing strong on the back nine of life. The first principle is:

Boldness Is Absolutely Necessary

There is a philosophy of boldness—to take advantage of every tiny opening towards victory.

Arnold Palmer

Life should be viewed as a challenge, not a threat. Though aging, difficult circumstances, or overwhelming responsibilities may force us to change some of our activities and plans, we should never abandon our efforts to meet the challenges that are set before us. Caleb didn't! He never relinquished his vision for the things God was committed to do.

Caleb refused to be limited by his age. At eighty-five, his enthusiasm was alive and thriving! He boldly sought to achieve great things for God. While many people his age would be content to position their rocking chair on the porch as their only activity, Caleb reminded Joshua to finish the relocation plans set into motion by Moses. No doubt, the forty-year trek in the wilderness brought moments of discouragement into Caleb's life. Do you think he had days when he wanted to quit, give in, or sell out? You bet! We've all experienced tough times and grueling assignments that left us wondering if we could make it another day. But we can follow the example of Caleb, whom the Bible says *wholeheartedly* followed the Lord despite forty discouraging years in the desert (Joshua 14:7-9).

114

The older we get, the less courage we tend to have. Repeated encounters with rejection, hurt feelings, and criticism cause us to draw in our wings of assertiveness. We don't venture far from home. We take fewer risks or no risks and justify it by saying that we are more mature. Experience has taught us to be more careful. But being careful isn't synonymous with stagnating. It appears that at eighty-five years of age, Caleb hadn't lost one ounce of his courage. He was ready for bigger risks than ever before. He refused to give up. He saw an unfinished task, and with a growing determination he sought to complete it.

Finishing strong requires that. On the golf course, at the office, in the kitchen, with the family, or through the neighborhood, life in God's kingdom demands boldness.

There's a second lesson from Caleb:

Age Is Irrelevant to Improvement

The man who says he's too old to learn new things probably always was.

Source unknown

Earl Woods is a retired military man who spent twenty years in the air force, with two tours of duty in Vietnam and one in Thailand. He's on the back nine of his life. When most people would have been settling in on retirement, Earl devoted countless hours to developing perhaps the world's greatest golfer, his son Tiger. Now he's grooming another prodigy, his eight-year-old granddaughter, Cheyenne. According to Earl, she's going to be "the Tiger of the LPGA tour" someday. Until then, Earl plans to enjoy the wild ride with his son, keeping him centered and balanced, and hoping that from time to time they can find a moment to catch their breath.

During a pastors' meeting I (Gary) attend each year with a group of close colleagues, several of us were discussing our response to new thoughts and ideas. One of my good friends, who was still leading a growing church at age seventy-three, said, "Well, I figure if I don't like it, it's probably the thing to do." This is a guy who isn't allowing himself to be intimidated by change, by the fact that he's growing older.

Many of us view aging as a process of withdrawal. We lose our energy. Our earning power diminishes. New ideas tend to be abrasive to us.

It doesn't have to be that way. Consider, for example, that presidents Ronald Reagan and George Bush were well into retirement age during their respective administrations, yet they had a basketful of ideas for improving our country and sought tirelessly to implement them.

As a matter of fact, it is possible for some of life's greatest achievements to occur during the retirement years. For instance, if memory serves us correctly, Colonel Sanders started the Kentucky Fried Chicken franchise at age sixty-five. The point: Age should never be an obstacle to improvement.

We were inspired by a news story of an illiterate, one-hundred-and-ten-year-old woman in Buenos Aires, Argentina, who enrolled in courses to learn how to read and write, saying she needed to better prepare herself for the challenges of the twenty-first century. What an inspiration!

At eighty-five years of age, Caleb was pushing to collect on the promise God had made to him forty-five years earlier—not to revel in his past, but to change his future. He believed he was just as ready, just as responsible, and just as capable to deal with it at eighty-five as he was at forty. Listen to him: "Now, as you can see, the Lord has kept me alive and well as he promised for all these forty-five years since Moses made this promise—even while Israel wandered in the wilderness. Today I am eighty-five years old. I am as strong now as I was when Moses sent me on that journey, and I can still travel and fight as well as I could then" (Joshua 14:10-11).

Caleb envisioned his future to be larger and of greater value than his past. His days may have been numbered, but not his vision. Here's a guy whose birthday didn't include a cake that read "Over the Hill." He was ready to take the hill! His vision and vitality for what was coming in his future remained as young and vibrant as Dick Clark's face. We don't see him trying to retire from his relationship with the Lord or the responsibility God wanted him to maintain. He wasn't looking for a condo on the Mediterranean, where his activities would consist of golf in the morning and bridge at night. We see confidence, abiding faith in God, and an undiminished vision.

Can you say that today, more than ever before, you are a person with confidence, an abiding faith in God, and an undiminished vision for what God is going to do in your life in the coming years?

Is it possible that you've allowed your age or circumstances to convince you that learning and improving are no longer necessary in your life? Have you become comfortable—financially, relationally, or perhaps spiritually? Are you content to stay where you are?

We asked ourselves these questions while writing this chapter and we are thrilled to be able to say that at ages fifty-two and thirty-four we are holding on to the hopes and dreams God has placed in our hearts. Our futures with God far outweigh all of our past experiences put together. Sometimes we have to fight off anxiety and doubts, but we are convinced that God is going to achieve far greater things *with* us and *through* us in the years ahead. As legendary baseball pitcher Satchel Paige said, "Age is a case of mind over matter. If you don't mind, it don't matter."

No matter what our age, there's always room for improvement. And if we plan to finish strong on the back nine of life, we must keep improving.

A third challenge from the story of Caleb:

Courage Is Nonnegotiable

Be on guard. Stand true to what you believe. Be courageous. Be strong.

1 CORINTHIANS 16:13

Who's the most courageous person to have ever lived? We think it was the first individual to eat an egg. Think about it! Can you imagine someone saying, "See what just fell out of that chicken over there? I'm going to crack it open, and whatever is inside I'm going to eat." That's raw courage!

Over and over again the Bible calls us to be people of courage. We are to be people who respond courageously on such a regular basis that it becomes second nature to us. When that happens, every day becomes an exciting adventure with God. As a matter of fact, it's a nonnegotiable issue for those who have a friendship with him. Consider these great promises: Deuteronomy 31:8 says, "Do not be afraid or discouraged, for the Lord is the one who goes before you. He will be with you; he will neither fail you nor forsake you." Then there's Joshua 1:9: "I command you—be strong and courageous! Do not be afraid or discouraged. For the Lord your God is with you wherever you go."

Caleb was a man of courage. As we continue to visit his life in the Bible, we see no indication of fear, withdrawal, or anxiety, even though he asked for the hill country in Canaan—the piece of land that was most difficult to secure. Read his words: " 'So I'm asking you to give me the hill country that the Lord promised me. You will remember that as scouts we found the Anakites living there in great, walled cities. But if the Lord is with me, I will drive them out of the land, just as the Lord said.' So Joshua blessed Caleb son of Jephunneh and gave Hebron to him as an inheritance" (Joshua 14:12-13).

Tell us that isn't a strong expression of courage! Caleb refused to allow forty years in the wilderness to break his spirit. He didn't cower or bow out simply because he was getting older. His faith in God's presence and God's performance had so much history to it that a life of courage was a natural by-product. His inspiration pushes through every age.

How would you rank yourself when it comes to courage? Do you have more or less than you used to have? How quick are you to respond to new promptings from God—to his calls to serve or to go where you've not been? Exhibiting courage is risky

119

but worth it, as pointed out in this anonymous quote from *Illustrations Unlimited:*

> To laugh is to risk appearing the fool. To weep is to risk appearing sentimental. To reach out for another is to risk involvement. To expose feelings is to risk exposing our true self. To place ideas and dreams before the crowd is to risk loss. To love is to risk not being loved in return. To live is to risk dying. To hope is to risk despair. To try at all is to risk failure. But risk we must, because the greatest hazard in life is to risk nothing. The man, the woman who risks nothing does nothing, has nothing, is nothing.

Regardless of age or circumstance, courage is a nonnegotiable if we intend to finish strong on the back nine of life.

The final requirement for finishing strong:

Kingdom Work Never Ends

Work for the Lord . . . the pay isn't much, but the retirement plan is out of this world.
Sign in a church office

Several months ago I (Gary) called my parents just to check up with them. When they answered the phone I said, "Where have you been?"

Actually, I didn't know that they had been any-where. I was just being funny. But the answer I got stunned me: "We just got home from church. We've been working in the after-school program for grade school kids."

Since they are in their seventies, I said, "What are you doing that for?"

"Well, son," my dad responded, "a program like that needs a lot of help. We want to be supportive, so we volunteered to be registrars and hall monitors."

Kingdom work never ends!

If we plan to finish life's back nine in a powerful way, we need to guard against the attitude that says, *I give up—I quit—it's time to retire.* We may not be able to stay in our careers past age sixty-five, but a change in career plans doesn't mean retiring from service to the Lord. Changes in health, marital status, living arrangements, parenting roles, or relationships may alter what we do or the way in which we do it, but it should never cause us to stop serving God.

You know what we've discovered? Many people retire from their commitment to kingdom work long before their body says they should. It's an attitude thing, just like it was for the twelve spies Israel sent to check out the land of Canaan. Seeing "giants" living there killed their positive attitude about occupying the land God had promised to them.

For many of us, the giants are in our thoughts. Our kids grow up and leave home, we reach a plateau in our careers, grandkids start popping up, we encounter the untimely death of family member or close friend, we experience a major financial setback—and suddenly we begin to pull in the wings of vision.

What giants are intimidating you? Maybe somebody standing next to you in the choir has criticized your voice, and you feel like quitting. Maybe
the junior high kids have been acting kind of
squirrelly lately, and you've decided not to
chaperone at that retreat after all. Maybe the child-
like behavior of an elderly relative is making you
uncomfortable, and you're tempted to abandon
your efforts to visit the nursing home. But people
like Caleb don't let those things keep them from
pushing on and finishing strong.

For many of us, getting older is a giant of discouragement that threatens to keep us from finishing strong. And in fact, we may face certain
limitations in terms of the type of service we are able
to perform. We may not be able to get down on the
floor with a two-year-old and roll around, but we
can still hold and care for a newborn in a rocking
chair in the nursery. Maybe our physical limitations
keep us from serving with junior highers. Maybe we
find ourselves confined to a wheelchair or walker,
but we could sure pick up our intensity with prayer
on behalf of those who are doing it. Maybe we can't
handle the stress of working with elementary school
children anymore, but we could sure do a great job
of writing notes of encouragement to them or to
those who lead them.

Furthermore, once our children grow up and
leave home, we have time for new kinds of adven-
tures. Suddenly, we can carve out an entire week
for a missions trip. And raising the money is a

whole lot easier when there are fewer mouths to feed at home.

We need to follow the example of Caleb, who refused to be intimidated or discouraged by giants—despite his age, his perception of his limited gifts, or his difficult circumstances. Nothing could destroy Caleb's willingness to serve the Lord enthusiastically until his death.

If we plan to finish strong in the back nine of life, we need to remember that kingdom work never ends. There's nothing in our spiritual contract with God that says we can stop serving.

Maybe you played poorly on the front nine of your life. Perhaps mistakes, broken dreams, missed opportunities, and a host of poor choices plagued your first round. You may be wondering if it's worth staying on the course. You might be feeling like the woman in the commercial who said, "I've fallen and I can't get up."

123

If so, remember this: The next shot is a fresh start. Tomorrow is a new day with a new opportunity. Get up and press on! Draw close to God, and watch him turn life around for you. The back nine is worth playing.

When I (Ken) am ready to quit, I try to inspire myself to keep going by reliving one of my most embarrassing moments. A few years ago, 7,000 people were gathered at Redbird Arena on the campus of Illinois State University for our church's annual Easter service. When it came time for me to speak, I made my way up the stairs toward the platform. My toe caught on the final step—I tripped and just about fell flat on my face. Everyone in the arena laughed as the bottom of my sport coat completely covered my head.

If you have never experienced 7,000 people laughing at you, get a root canal first—it's less painful! Actually, when the laughter died down I said, "Have you ever had one of those dreams where you do something stupid in front of thousands of people?" Then came my moment of redemption. I said, "It's not that bad." I had the last laugh that day as we all laughed together.

If you are stumbling through a back nine of life, allow yourself to be inspired by Caleb. Be bold and courageous. Don't allow age or past defeats or overwhelming responsibilities to discourage you. Remember that kingdom work never ends. And never forget that the stroke of the Master's hand is painting a picture—a beautiful portrait of your life that will end victoriously. Whether on the golf course or in life, don't give up—never, ever give up!

Today's round is finished. We want to leave you with these words of advice: Whatever you set out to accomplish, give it all you've got, and keep your eyes focused keenly on the Lord—and your goal. Tomorrow is a new day with a new opportunity.

To put it in golf terms—tee it up with God tomorrow. Remain patient. Trust your swing. Stay focused. Put the ball in play, and keep your life squarely in Christ. It will create far more opportunities to finish strong.

Selected Bibliography

Anderson, Peggy, compiler. *Great Quotes from Great Leaders.*
Lombard, Ill.: Celebrating Excellence, Great Quotations,
Inc., 1989.

Blanchard, Ken. "Church in the 21st Century." In *Next* 4,
no. 3 (August 1994).

Canfield, Jack, Mark Victor Hansen, and Barry Spilchuck.
A Cup of Chicken Soup for the Soul. Deerfield Beach, Fla.: Health
Communications, Inc., 1996.

Carroll, Jeff. *Bible Illustrator.* Index no. 1764 & 3242.
Hiawatha, Iowa: Parsons Technology, 1994.

Chambers, Oswald. *My Utmost for His Highest.* Ed. James G.
Reimann. Grand Rapids: Discovery House Publishers, 1992.

Coop, Dr. Richard. *Mind Over Golf.* Old Tappen, N.J.:
MacMillan Publishing Company, 1993.

Dupree, Max. *Leadership Is an Art.* New York: Dell Publishing
Co., 1990.

Dyet, James. *Out of the Rough.* Nashville: Thomas Nelson
Publishers, 1996.

Freeman, Criswell. *The Golfer's Book of Wisdom.* Nashville:
Walnut Grove Press, 1995.

Goldwyn, Samuel. *Injoy Life Club* 9, no. 10 (April, 1994).

Hewett, James S. *Illustrations Unlimited.* Wheaton, Ill.: Tyndale House Publishers, Inc. 1988.

Liebman, Glenn. *Golf Shorts.* Lincolnwood, Ill.: Contemporary Books, 1995.

McKenzie, E. C. *14,000 Quips and Quotes.* Ada, Mich.: Baker Books, 1993.

Maxwell, John. *The Winning Attitude.* San Bernardino, Calif.: Here's Life Publishers, 1991.

Nelson, Kevin. *The Golfer's Book of Daily Inspiration.* Lincolnwood, Ill.: Contemporary Books, 1996.

Nicklaus, Jack. *Golf My Way.* New York: Simon & Schuster, 1976.

Olman, John M., and Morton W. Olman. *The Encyclopedia of Golf Collectibles.* Iola, Wis.: Books Americana, 1985.

Penick, Harvey. *And If You Play Golf, You're My Friend.* New York: Simon & Schuster, 1993.

Phillips, Emo. *E=MO.* CBS Records, 1985.

Sherman, Ed. "Don't Count on a Norman Conquest." *Chicago Tribune,* 6 April 1997.

Swindoll, Chuck. *Growing Deep in the Christian Life.* Sisters, Ore.: Multnomah Press, 1986.

Swindoll, Chuck. Remarks made at the Conference on Biblical Exposition. Houston, Tex. March 7-10, 1988.

Swindoll, Chuck. *Strengthening Your Grip.* Waco, Tex: Word Publishers, 1982.

About the Authors

Gary York and Ken Osness are pastors at Eastview Christian Church, a 3,000-member congregation in Bloomington, Illinois. Gary, senior pastor at Eastview, has authored articles for such periodicals as *Christian Standard* and *Lookout.* He is a conference and seminar leader and has a national tape ministry. Ken is pastor of community impact and a member of the teaching team at Eastview.